Wonderful
ways with
Wax

Wonderful
ways with
Wax

ENCAUSTIC ART FOR CRAFT PROJECTS

Jann Visser

SEARCH PRESS

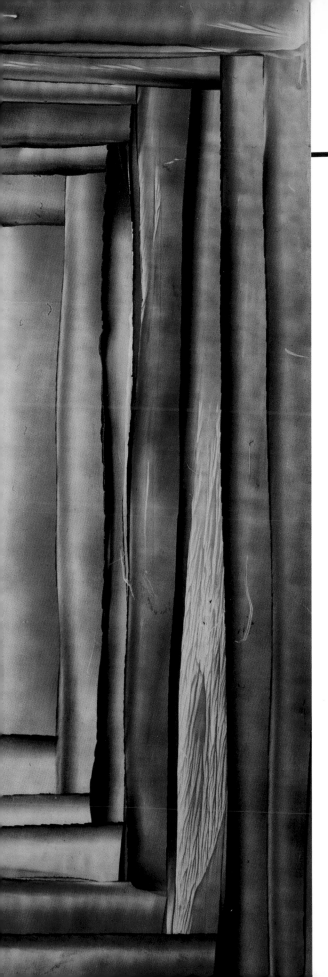

Contents

First published in Great Britain 2011
Search Press Limited
Wellwood, North Farm Road,
Tunbridge Wells, Kent, TN2 3DR

Originally published in South Africa in 2011 by Metz Press
1 Cameronians Ave, Welgemoed 7530, South Africa

Copyright © Metz Press 2011
Copyright text and designs © Jann Visser

Publisher	Wilsia Metz
Editor	Deborah Morbin
Proofreader	Francie Botes
Photographer	Ivan Naudé
Design and lay-out	Liezl Maree
Printed and bound in Singapore by Tien Wah Press	
ISBN	978-1-84448-790-5

Introduction

Meet the challenge ... discover the fun

The minute I saw a demonstration on Encaustic Art, I was hooked. I remember standing with my eyes as big as saucers and my mouth wide open, thinking to myself, "If I hadn't seen it with my own eyes I would not have believed it". To create something so beautiful in a matter of minutes fascinated me, especially since I was used to painting in oils and having to wait until the painting was dry, which took weeks! In our busy, modern lives it's good to know that there is an 'instant' art and encaustic painting is just that: an ideal medium for today's fast pace. Since you work with liquid wax colours, which cool immediately, lengthy drying time is certainly not a factor. Encaustic paintings can be reworked over and over, months (or even years) later, by the simple addition of heat.

Encaustic painting was developed by the ancient Greeks more than 2000 years ago; the Greek word for encaustic is *encaustikos*, which means 'to heat' or 'burn in'. Encaustic paint consists of beeswax, resin and pigment. This wax can be adhered to a number of supports such as print paper, card, a good quality photo paper, ceramic, canvas and wood. Wax has several inherent qualities: it is a natural adhesive that is moisture, mildew, fungus and insect resistant. As encaustic paints do not contain oils, they will not yellow or darken with age, making them perhaps the most durable form of painting. (This is evident from the Faiyum mummy portraits in Egypt that have survived for more than 2000 years without deteriorating whatsoever. The colour of the wax remains as fresh as the day the paintings were created.) Another advantage of encaustic paint is that it is solvent free, which means that there is no need for turpentine and mineral spirits.

Encaustic work is unique in that, because of the luminosity of the wax, it delivers colour in a way no other medium can. Unlike traditional paint (oil, acrylics), light passes through the translucent layers and is reflected back to the surface, creating luminosity. Layers of wax are fused and bonded together by heating or 'burning in'.

The following information was taken from the script for my appearance on the television programme, Top Billing, which was aired in September 2009.

"When you consider that bees must fly a distance of an estimated six times around the earth to yield half a kilogram of this precious wax, you get to realise that this is a touch more special than simply painting with a watercolour kit. Without bees to produce this golden product, few things would get pollinated, plants would stop reproducing and making food, and pretty soon life, and encaustic art, would grind to a halt."

I believe that encaustic art will encourage you to view painting differently and enhance your powers of creativity. I'm sure that you'll be surprised to discover how quickly and skilfully you'll master painting with wax.

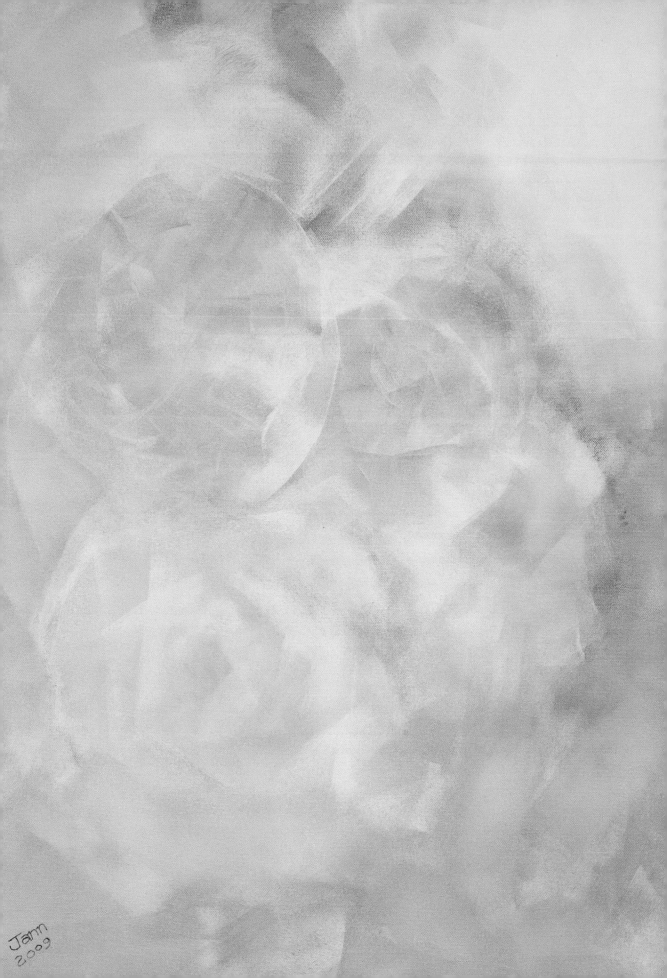

Equipment

The following items are needed for this craft. Don't worry, you don't have to rush out and buy everything at once, especially since some of the equipment mentioned replaces others. Rather, read through the list of equipment and their uses and then start building up your collection, as new items are needed for different projects. Obviously, some of the items will be used constantly, so there will be an initial outlay in order to get started.

Encaustic iron

It is a thermostatically controlled electric iron, weighing just over 500 g (or 1 lb), that can be used either at 120V – 120W 60Hz or 240V – 240W 50Hz. It has a temperature dial that can be adjusted and a detachable handle that can be clipped over the iron, making it very compact. Getting to know the iron:

1. Assembling the iron

2. Handle attached

3. Temperature settings

4. Using the iron as a hot plate

5. Cable position

6. Holding the iron pointed down

7. Holding the iron for edge marking

8. Cleaning the iron

Stylus

This is like a heated pen, which is used for adding finer details to a picture. It is set at a low temperature and cannot be adjusted. The stylus has various attachments that are interchangeable and used for different effects, such as drawing, brush, micro (like a baby iron), mini (a small triangle) and round tips. They are attached by undoing the screw on the side of the stylus.

Drawing tip

The drawing tip is used to draw objects such as birds, trees, fences, posts, dragonflies or any other fine detail that you may want to add to your artwork. To use, allow to heat and load the tip with wax. Dab off excess wax on your backing paper.

Brush tip

This is versatile in that it gives you a few options. It is a useful tip to use when adding leaves to your trees or drawing fir trees. Depending on how you use it, you can make long brush-like strokes, as in a fir tree, or stipple the brush to create leaves on a standard tree. It's up to you to decide how full you want your tree to look.

Micro-iron tip

The micro-iron tip can be used for little butterflies, flowers or a small kaleidoscope picture. The tip can also be used to add foliage or to make changes in specific places on your picture. This is because the heated area is small enough not to touch the rest of the surrounding picture.

Mini-iron tip

The mini-iron tip is used for bigger versions of images created with the micro-iron tip, as well as for abstract designs.

Round tip

This is ideal for grapes, balloons and other round shapes such as suns and moons. It also makes a lovely border or can be used for circles incorporated into any abstract design.

Travelling iron

A travelling iron can be used as a substitute for the encaustic iron, although it is advisable to use the correct equipment for this art. Ensure that no steam is used when working with the travelling iron and set the temperature at a minimum temperature similar to that of a silk setting. However, you will have to experiment as irons vary. Some travelling irons have small holes on the base plate, which doesn't really work; ideally you should try to find one with a solid base plate. If you are experimenting with an iron that has holes in the base and wax ends up inside one of the holes, you can take a toothpick and a tissue to remove the unwanted wax while the iron is still hot.

There are larger domestic irons that have a solid base plate; however, these are big and hard to handle and controlling the temperature is often tricky.

So when substituting a piece of equipment it must be used with caution and, because the replacement is not a genuine encaustic iron, you will have to experiment before moving directly on to a project. You also need to be aware that the end result will differ from the one you would achieve if you used the genuine product.

HINT: Soldering irons and wood burning tools (called pyrography tools) are not suitable as they get far too hot and scorch the wax.

Hot tray

This can be used in a couple of different ways but remember, like the iron, the temperature setting should also always be kept low. When using brushes for a larger painting, the hot tray can be useful in keeping your brushes warm between applications of different colours, as well as being used to melt larger amounts of wax for bigger pictures. You will have to work reasonably quickly when using the melted wax from the hot tray.

Hairdryer

A hairdryer is used to blow the wax around – either on card or canvas – keeping it melted. Beautiful effects are created with this technique, depending how close or how far away you hold the hairdryer. Heat guns and paint strippers can be used with caution but, even then, only if you have had experience with this type of equipment.

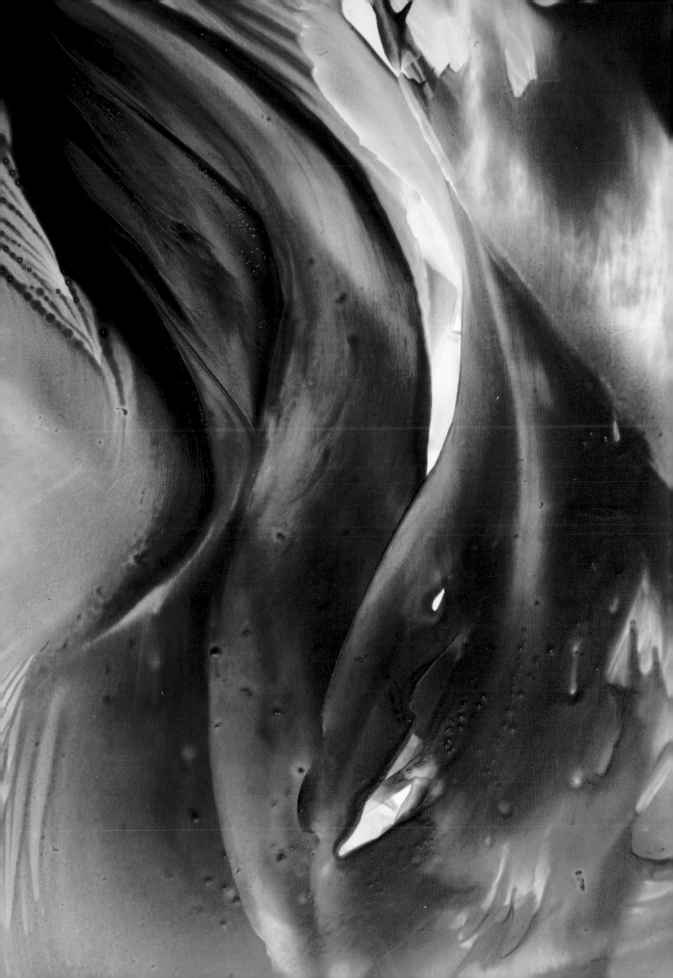

Paintbrushes

Though some other paintbrushes can be used, hog's hair brushes give the best results. Nylon brushes are not recommended as they may melt in the hot wax. Natural brushes are ideal for both dabbing and creating brush stroke styles with the melted wax. For larger pieces of work and larger brushes (about 20 mm in width), it is best to use small tins to heat and contain the waxes, for example small food tins, foil cases or old cupcake tins. It's advisable to use several brushes to avoid constant cleaning. You can roughly clean waxed-covered brush fibres whilst still warm, using a soft tissue. For more thorough cleaning, mineral turpentine or white spirits can be used, but do this in a well-ventilated room, away from all heating tools, as these solvents are highy flammable.

Scriber

A scriber is made of metal and is used to scrape off the wax from your picture to form, for example, a river. The scriber can be substituted with toothpicks or a knitting needle, or really anything suitable for scraping away wax.

Permanent markers

These are used for drawing, creating borders around your artwork or adding silhouettes.

Gold pens

They can be used to either highlight certain areas or add dragonflies, birds or grasses.

Gold powder

Use a small brush to add little amounts of gold powder to your work in order to create a little shimmer to water.

Wax

All encaustic art waxes are inter-mixable. Wax must be warmed on a heat-controlled device around 80 °C (180 °F) and applied whilst hot. The pigment in some of the wax is strong and will come out darker or more intense, so caution should be taken when using these colours. As a guide, the opaque, pastel or milky colours are not as strong in pigment as the rest of the colours. Pearlescent wax can be added to various transparent colours to create an entire new range of different hues.

Buffing material

Soft tissue or a soft, lint-free fabric is essential to buff your work when completed. This gives the dry wax a lovely sheen, enhancing the colour.

Wax sealer

This is a protective coating for any wax art or mixed media. This coating will keep your artwork looking fresh and bright. The ideal brush to use in order to apply wax sealer is a soft flat, 2 cm (¾ in) watercolour brush and the surface should be coated in one direction only. The completed artwork must be polished with a soft cloth as this enables even spread and optimal adhesion of the wax sealer.

To create a glazing effect, add dry pigment or acrylic colours to the sealer as this transforms it into workable acrylic paint. Thin the glaze with up to 20% water and leave your work to dry to a satin, wax-like finish for approximately 2 hours. After use, clean brushes with warm water.

Metal pots

It is unsafe to use very small pieces of wax when creating a picture, as you could easily burn your fingers when applying them to the hot base of the iron. To create a bigger block of wax I melt these small pieces together in the little metal pots that normally contain tea lights. Collect bits of wax of the same colour and pop into the pots (after removing any remaining candle wax), which have been placed onto an iron in the 'hot plate' position. Allow the wax to melt completely, grab each little pot with long-nose pliers and pour the wax into a small paper cup case (available from baking shops). Allow to harden and peel away the paper cup before you use the wax. This method can be used to create your own colours too.

HINT: Do not discard the bits of candle wax you remove from these pots – it can be used to clean your encaustic iron.

Sponge roller

This is used together with the hot tray and a hairdryer. The high density sponge on the roller soaks up the wax that has been melted on the hot tray. This wax in the sponge cools instantly so the hairdryer is used to keep the wax liquid. The hairdryer is set to a high heat, high speed and held over the roller, as you move the roller up and down the canvas, thus releasing the wax. This method of transferring wax works well on a framed canvas, and the result is an even, smooth coat of wax.

Supports

These are the 'bases' on which you will work. Some of them can be used as is, others will need a little preparation.

Card

A sealed, lightweight card is suitable. This can be white or coloured, and of varying sizes; it all depends on the type of picture you are creating. White card reflects the translucent colours effectively, leaving a beautiful, vibrant and permanent enamel appearance. This card needs no preparation and offers a good base for smaller work.

Canvas

You can use either loose, coated canvas or a ready-made, stretched, coated canvas on a wooden frame.

Ceramic

Bisque items can be decorated with a stylus or paintbrushes and wax.

Ostrich eggs

Once decorated, these eggs look beautiful. A stylus is used to decorate the eggs, as the flat, hard base of the iron doesn't work at all well on a rounded surface. You could also apply the wax blocks directly onto the egg in order to add layers and subtle tones to the design.

Board

For larger work, MDF (Medium Density Fibre or Superwood) board is recommended. The naturally absorbent surface can be used, but it is advisable to rather prime the surface with a diluted mix as this reduces the amount of wax needed. Use 30% white wood glue diluted with 70% water and coat *both* sides of the MDF board as this makes it more stable. Once treated, the board should still be absorbent and this primed surface is ideally suited for the wax. When working on the board, heat it first with a hot air gun. Once warmed, the encaustic wax will remain workable for longer.

Colour wheel

The sequence of colours on a colour wheel should resemble that of the rainbow. It is an excellent tool to help understand colour balance and harmony for use in painting, as well as interior decorating and commercial use.

Primary colours
- Red
- Yellow
- Blue

Secondary colours
- Orange (mix red + yellow)
- Green (mix yellow + blue)
- Purple (mix blue + red)

Tertiary colours
- Yellow-orange
- Red-violet
- Blue-green
- Red-orange
- Blue-violet
- Yellow-green

A tertiary colour is obtained when you mix a primary colour red, yellow or blue with its adjacent secondary colour. For example, if you mix the primary colour yellow with the secondary colour orange, yellow-orange would be the tertiary colour.

Complementary colours

You will find these colours opposite each other on the colour wheel. Examples would be: blue/orange, purple/yellow and red/green. You will notice that when they are placed next to each other, they contrast with one another.

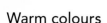

Warm colours

Refer to the colour chart below. Warm colours range from yellows to oranges through to reds and browns. In painting, these colours are often used in the foreground.

Cool colours

Refer to the colour chart below. Cool colours range from pastel blue, ultramarine blue, indigo, lilac and turquoise through to leaf, sap and olive green. For instance, cool blue hues indicate distance in a landscape that depicts horizons, sky and clouds.

The following colours are available:

Warm colour chart

5 Lemon yellow

4 Golden yellow

30 Pastel orange

34 Pastel coral

24 Pink

2 Vermillion

3 Orange

43 Bright red

1 Crimson

12 Red violet

13 Rust brown

22 Umbre brown

21 Venetian red

20 Yellow ochre

28 Bronze metallic

25 Gold metallic

Cool colour chart

31 Pastel blue

19 Cobalt blue

10 Ultramarine blue

9 Blue

18 Prussian blue

47 Indigo

32 Pastel lilac

11 Blue violet

45 Sap green

8 Blue green

6 Leaf green

7 Green

23 Olive green

Techniques

There are basically four techniques used for this art. As you become more familiar with them, you can adapt them to your particular style.

Smoothing

The first technique is called 'smooth-ing'. The smoothing technique is used for skies, lakes, hills or anything that has an uninterrupted, smooth flow of wax. When using this method, it is very important to remember that the pressure you use when gliding the iron over the card is light and smooth, not jerky. The speed is important too: Glide the iron slowly when laying the wax because if you go fast it almost *removes* the wax. In other words, one constant, slow movement from beginning to end. By doing this, you achieve an even layer of wax.

1. Loading the iron

2. Gliding colour over

Load the base of the iron with the chosen colours of wax, then turn the iron over and place it onto the card, gliding the iron from one side to the other, making sure that the iron is completely off the card.

1

2

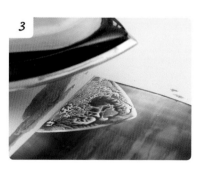

3

4

Lifting

The lifting technique is used for foli-age in a landscape or, for example, coral in an underwater scene. It can also be used purely as an interesting design in an abstract artwork. First load the base of the iron with the chosen colours of wax, then place the iron onto the area of the card where you would like the effect and simply lift the iron off the card. The result is determined by the speed with which you lift the iron off the card, as well as the amount of wax that you use. A vacuum is formed when you lift the iron off the card, causing air to rush in between the wax, leaving behind a lined, feathery effect.

Edge marking

The edge marking technique is used for creating thin lines. These thin lines can either form long grasses in a landscape or small tufts of grass, depending on the length, or lines in an abstract. How thick or thin your lines come out depends on how straight you glide the iron over the wax. These lines are not actually drawn onto the card; they are formed by using the side or edge of the iron which moves the wax away, revealing the white card underneath. This is really effective because the lines have a dark side which gives them dimension. If you slide the iron slightly to one side when creating these lines, you will get a thicker line.

Load the base of the iron with some wax. Smooth it over the card. Turn the iron onto its side, with the handle facing you and glide it from the bottom of the card towards the top.

Note: You may find it easier to hold the iron with the handle facing away from you, using the opposite side of the iron, but from experience, I have found that you have less control this way.

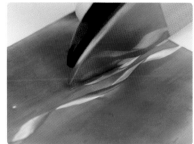

1. Squiggle

2. Straight

3. Bush

4. Starburst

5. Criss-cross

Non-iron techniques

The great thing about painting with wax is that you can do many other projects without the use of the encaustic or travelling iron and stylus. You really just have to think of ways to melt wax. The basic techniques remain the same, and their application is explained in the relevant projects.

Projects

Read these general guidelines before you start ...

Unless otherwise stated, at the beginning of each project – when using the iron – ensure that it is switched on and set at the **low** temperature before you start. If using the stylus, it too must be switched on – and hot – before you begin using it. Both of these take about five minutes to heat up.

Always clean the equipment thoroughly when you have finished your picture. Clean the iron with a clear candle melted onto the bottom of the hot iron and wipe off with some tissue. Wax runs down the side of the iron and gathers at the bottom of its base, so it is extremely important to remove the wax from this area, otherwise you may find the wax will suddenly blob onto your artwork without you noticing. Use a toothpick and some tissue to clean up.

To clean the tip of the stylus, gently dip it into some clear candle wax and wipe with a soft tissue or cloth.

Clean backing paper should be laid down at the start of each project: 48.8 gsm unprinted newspaper or computer paper works well. Unprinted newspaper is actually referred to as plain newsprint; however, as that sounds rather contradictory, I decided that it's easier to refer to it as unprinted newspaper. Don't be tempted to use printed newspaper because the ink may be transferred to your artwork. I also place a thick, bull denim tablecloth underneath the backing paper.

Each project is 'buffed' with a soft tissue when finished. Work back and forth, using light strokes and taking care not to rub too hard as this could result in the removal of some of the wax or smudging of your work. When done, seal with wax sealer. If you want to rework your picture at a later stage, leave the wax sealer off until you are quite sure that you are finished.

Note: It is always advisable to use the correct products, for example wax sealer, but if you want to experiment with sealers like podge (water-based varnish) and polyurethane varnish, use them with caution. If you use podge to seal your artwork, ensure that it is not too thick and is completely dry before touching it. Do not put anything on top of your work as this may result in the podge sticking to it and peeling off the picture.

Abstracts

Creating abstracts with encaustic is unpredictable. Nothing is pre-planned so it is the surprise element and vivid colours of wax that make these abstracts beautiful and intriguing.

Rhythmic abstract

The great thing about doing this type of abstract is that the iron leaves a definite trail of wax, thereby creating a 'drag' line. What actually happens is that when you stop and start, the iron removes a little wax off the card, exposing the white card underneath it. Two complementary colours work well with this type of picture.

Requirements

- Backing paper
- Iron
- Any two waxes – like red violet and ultramarine blue
- White A6 card

1. Prepare your work area by placing backing paper onto the table.

HINT: You must have a flat surface, as the iron will detect any lumps or bumps under the card. This is because the iron can't follow contours as it has a flat, hard surface.

2. Turn the iron onto the low setting and face the base upwards. Always keep the iron **horizontal** because when wax is melted, it will run off if you tilt the iron. Something to remember is that light-coloured waxes run easier than the darker ones.

3. Take one of your chosen colours and touch it slightly onto the base of the iron. The longer you hold the wax, the more it will melt. Repeat with your second colour.

4. Turn the iron over and place it on the card. Hold the card at the corners with your other hand and move from left to right (or right to left if you are left-handed). This first stage covers the card with a layer of wax.

5. Now place the iron onto the card again, this time moving the iron in a semicircle over the wax with small jerking movements (about 2 mm apart), ensuring that you do not lift the iron off the card. A very interesting picture begins to form. Continue until you are happy with the result.

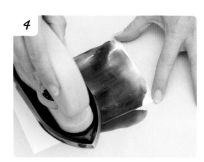

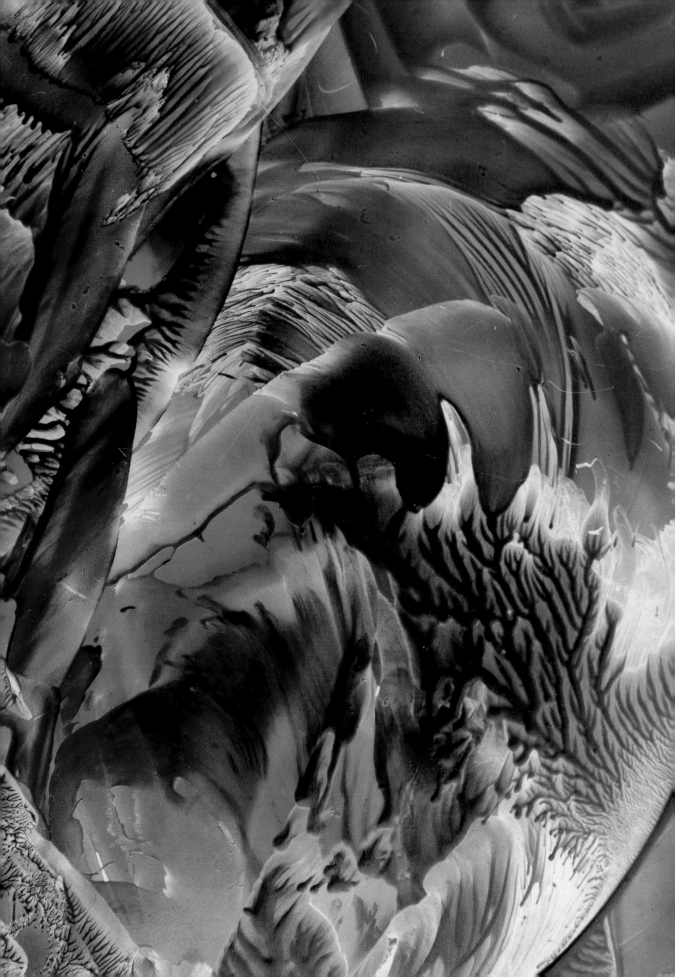

Chaotic abstract

For this effect, I sometimes take the card in my hand and work in the air. You may think that sounds strange but it's really fun creating a picture this way. However, you can lay the card flat on your work surface if you prefer to do so. The wax-loaded iron can be touched lightly on the card and pulled off leaving a beautiful pattern behind. This type of picture is very much like looking at clouds; after a while you begin to see things like animal forms or faces.

Requirements

- Iron
- Any two or three waxes
- White A6 card
- Tissue

1. Load the iron with two or three colours of wax.

2. Lay the base.

3. Hold the card in front of you (in the air) and press the iron onto the card, supporting the card with your other hand. As the iron touches the card, it sticks and by pulling the iron one way or another, and then off the card, the wax leaves a vein-like image behind.

4. Continue until you are happy with the result.

HINT: Be careful not to burn yourself. Keep your supporting hand away from the direct heat of the iron base.

5. Buff the picture lightly with the tissue.

HINT: Do not rub too hard as you will remove the wax from your card or you may even smudge your picture.

Wax drawing with tissue

I'm going to cover three ways in which to use tissue.
I like these methods because it is fun seeing what you can
do with tissue. It's also an ideal opportunity to use the
less common coloured waxes – like the fluorescent ones
– as they work well with the white card as a background.
However, you can also try these methods using dark card as
a base, and lighter or pastel waxes to create your artwork.

Requirements

- White A6 card
- Iron
- Tissue – 2 ply
- Any three or four waxes
- Hot tray
- Wax sealer

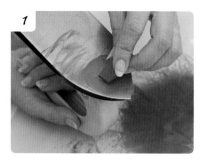

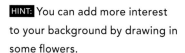

Method 1

1. You will first have to load your
wax onto the tissue, making sure
that you have applied enough.
Don't worry if you have to experiment a little; getting it right comes
with time and experience.

2. Assemble your iron like a mini
base plate. See notes on assembling
the iron on page 8.

3. Place your white card onto the
heated iron and, using the wax-
loaded tissue, make a few dabs.
As the tissue heats up, the wax will
begin to transfer from the tissue to
the card. In other words, the tissue
is acting like your paintbrush.

HINT: You can add more interest
to your background by drawing in
some flowers.

Method 2

1. With this method, you iron the
wax onto the card first. Simply lay
the wax anyhow, any way.

2. Now take the card and lay it on
the base plate of the iron or the hot
tray. It will melt easily and quickly so
you'll have to work fast when using
this method. Take the clean tissue,
gather it up and use the ends of
the tissue like a brush to create a
brushed effect.

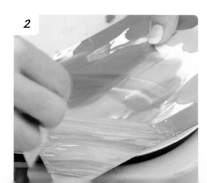

Method 3

1. Load the tissue with wax by melting one colour at a time onto the base of the iron and then transferring the wax onto the tissue. You will now work onto the card, which is placed on backing paper.

2. Place the loaded tissue over the card, holding it with one hand. Hold the iron in the other hand and slide the flat base of the iron over the tissue. What happens here is that the heat pushes the wax through the tissue and onto the card, leaving an imprint of the tissue that is very subtle and soft.

3. Reload the tissue with wax if you prefer a darker picture.

4. Edge mark over the tissue transferred wax, adding some colour to enhance the image if necessary.

5. Buff your picture with a soft, clean tissue.

HINT: You can also buff your picture with soft, t-shirt material if you happen to have any. This fabric can also be used to wipe your iron clean.

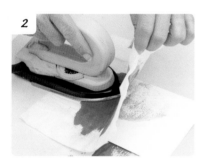

Wax through tissue

There are many ways of working with the wax. This method is unusual as the wax is pushed through the tissue leaving a tissue trail. Once you are experienced, you can actually draw a realistic picture using this method, but for now I will describe how to create an abstract picture.

Requirements

- Backing paper
- Tissue – 2-ply
- Any three waxes
- Iron
- White A6 card

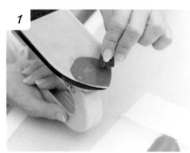

1. Place the tissue onto the backing paper and iron the first wax colour onto the tissue. Lift quickly so it does not stick to the backing paper. Repeat this process until you have used all three colours next to each other on the tissue.

2. Place the card onto the backing paper and the tissue onto the card, then iron over the tissue. Use the side of the iron to create score marks, solid, straight definite lines, lifting the tissue as you go to see what kind of picture unfolds. You can manoeuvre the iron in various directions to leave different tissue trails of wax pushed onto the card.

Note: If you want to create a realistic picture, follow the above steps until it comes to using the iron to create score marks. Instead, have a simple picture in mind and then try to *draw* the picture using only the edge of the iron (the iron is actually acting like a pencil or pen), lifting the tissue to see the result. This technique is rather difficult so only try it when you are quite adept at handling the iron.

Kaleidoscope

The transparent colours in this quick and easy project make it very effective. It also uses three waxes, though four colours appear because the iron occasionally lifts off all of the wax, exposing the white card underneath.

Requirements

- White A6 card
- Ruler
- Pencil
- Iron
- Any seven waxes

1. Find the centre of your card by placing the ruler diagonally from one corner to the other and drawing a very faint line of about 2 cm in the middle of the card. Repeat this process on the two opposite corners, resulting in a small pencil cross in the middle of the card. This can be done on either a square or a rectangle.

2. Load your iron with the lightest colour wax about 3 cm down from the tip of the iron. Now turn the iron over and place it in one of the quarters of the pencil cross, then lift it off slowly, pushing the nose down as you lift from the back. This is the 'lifting' technique that will be used throughout the project.

3. Without reloading the iron, do the same on the next quarter. Then reload with the same wax and repeat on the last two quarters. You will see that a line has formed in between each iron mark. On the next layer you will use the second lightest colour wax and place the iron on the formed line.

4. From here onwards, use your imagination as to where to place the iron, continuing in a circle and using the colours from light to dark. For example, on the fourth layer, you can load your iron with two different colours at once.

5. Fill in any gaps towards the end and make a border if you wish (see page 39).

HINT: Instead of just lifting the iron, try using a smoothing technique (see smoothing technique on page 18) on alternate layers or even create the whole kaleidoscope with the smoothing technique. This picture is effective using a light colour in the middle and gradually going darker as you work towards the outer edges.

4

4

5

Mandala

A mandala can best be described as a structured abstract that has a mirror image. These are usually done in the form of a circle but I have done this one on a square. The key to the success of this picture is balance and complementary colours. You can also use a printed picture of a mandala and fill in the design with various coloured waxes, using the stylus with different tips attached.

Requirements

- Square white card about 150 x 150 mm
- Iron
- Yellow, green, blue and red waxes
- Scriber or similar object to scratch off wax (not too sharp!)
- Tissue – 2 ply
- Printed picture of a mandala (optional)

1. Using your lightest colour wax, for example yellow, create the background.

HINT: Only load wax onto half of the iron, any more will just be wasted and end up on the backing paper.

2. Using your scriber, scratch a cross in the middle of your background. Place the point of the iron a few millimetres from the centre of the cross and lift it off, ensuring that your iron is square to the edge of the card. Repeat this on all four sides, creating images.

3. Next load the green wax onto the base of the iron. Place the iron between two existing images and wiggle towards the edge of the paper. Repeat all round.

4. Load with the red wax and try changing the technique to smoothing, using a small, wiggly, zigzag motion.

5. Lastly load with a dark blue and add a further eight images (big ones on the sides and small ones in the corners), but using straight lifts as your technique.

Note: If you have a bigger card, you can use more colours and add extra layers.

2

3

3

4

5

5

Sponge roller abstract on canvas

Requirements

- Canvas – any size
- Hot tray
- Coral, burgundy, yellow and white wax
- Hairdryer
- Small, high-density sponge roller with handle
- Cloth sheeting
- Stylus (optional)

The sponge roller is a great way of achieving a smooth, even coating (or background) on your canvas. Of course, the problem is that the roller is not a heated tool so you have to do things slightly differently in order to transfer the wax from the roller to the canvas.

1. Turn the hot tray to a low setting and melt a small amount of wax by smoothing the chosen colour directly onto the hot tray. Take your sponge roller and roll it over the wax. Melt some more wax and repeat until you have an even amount on the sponge.

2. Place the canvas on a cloth on the floor. (I like to work on the floor but you may prefer to work on the table.) Hold the roller in one hand and the hairdryer in the other. Turn the hairdryer onto high heat and speed and position it over the roller.

3. Begin to roll the roller – with the hairdryer directly over it – causing the hot blast of air to push through the roller and melt the wax directly onto the canvas. Sometimes you get what I call 'bald patches'. This happens because the roller sometimes lifts the wax up off the canvas. If this happens, simply keep going with the hot air and re-lay the wax down again.

4. Once you have created your background, you can then continue to either blow flowers or draw a picture with the stylus. Blown flowers look very nice on this type of artwork – see page 84.

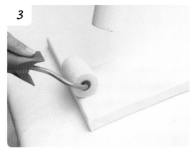

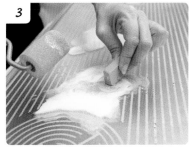

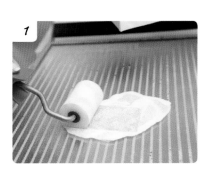

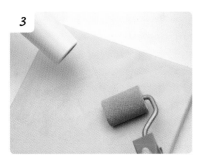

The completed canvas can be a work of art in its own right, or serve as a background for mounting a second artwork.

Upside-down abstract

The process here is reversed as the heat source is underneath the wax, creating a warm surface on which to work. The melted wax is then transferred from the surface onto the card, so the card becomes the painting tool!

Requirements

- Hot tray
- Any three waxes
- White A6 card
- Old credit card (optional)
- Old comb (optional)

1. Turn your hot tray onto a low setting. As these appliances vary, you may have to experiment with the temperature at first. There should be enough heat to melt the wax without it smoking.

2. Melt small amounts of each wax onto the hot tray.

3. Take your card and place it directly over the melted wax but keep a corner free in order to lift the card up. Press on top of the card with the other hand, turning it clockwise and anti-clockwise, which gives a stunning result. This technique is a mixture of the lifting and smoothing effect, but instead of doing it with the iron you are moving the card.

Abstract fish puzzle

Find a picture of a fish so that you can copy its shape or draw one yourself, creating a template. Use an old encaustic picture that you have previously discarded or create a new one specifically for this project. You are going to cut the shape out of the existing encaustic picture and attach it to a bigger card using raised, double-sided tape to give it depth.

Requirements

- Encaustic abstract(s)
- Fish template (page 126)
- Pencil
- Scissors
- Punch
- Raised, double-sided tape
- White A5 card (or bigger for mounting)

1. Trace the outline of the fish template onto the back of the encaustic picture and cut it out.

2. Use a punch to cut bubbles.

3. Decide where you would like the pieces to be positioned on the card and make a couple of small pencil marks to guide you.

4. Cut small pieces of double-sided tape and attach them to the back of the fish. Remove the cover tape and stick the pieces down securely. This picture can be board-mounted and hung on the wall.

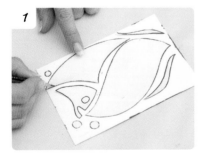

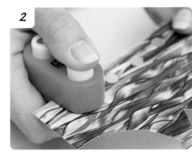

Borders

Adding a border around your artwork makes it look complete. (If you are placing your finished artwork in a framed card, it's not necessary to put a border around it, as it will get lost behind the cut-out frame.) These borders can be created 'plain' or 'designed'.

Plain borders

For a plain border, draw a pencil line about 1,5 cm in from the edges on all four sides, creating a frame. If you have already completed your picture, you will notice that the wax will peel off as your pencil glides through it, leaving a line. This is your guide, but you should try to hide the line when you create your border. Now all you do is simply slide the iron over the border, with the point of the iron following the pencil mark. If you run out of wax, take the same colour and load a small amount onto the base of the iron – about 2 cm from the tip down – and continue with your border. Try to use a continuous movement to prevent getting start/ stop lines.

Interesting borders

For a more interesting border, follow the previous step for a plain border and then add a different colour wax to the tip of the base, placing the point on the line (to make an arrow-head) then lift. Continue until you have gone all the way around your picture. You can also continue with another smaller row of arrowheads under the first row – it's entirely up to you. However, the best part of encaustic is that if you don't like the detailed border and would prefer to go back to the plain one, simply place the iron over the previous border and re-create your plain one!

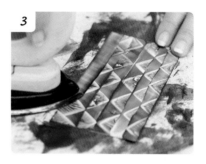

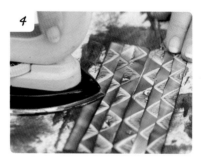

Landscapes

My favourite picture to demonstrate has to be the classic landscape. I love the reaction on people's faces when I do this picture. People look in absolute disbelief at the speed and detail achieved, as well as how instantly it dries. The landscape has many variants; for example, you could produce a soft sky by simply using lovely pastel colours or create a dynamic sky using the more dramatic sunset colours.

When planning the details of your landscape, you first decide on the type of sky, followed by the look of the hills and lastly what appears in the foreground.

I am going to give you a few examples of different landscape compositions, bearing in mind that these can be changed and mixed to your liking.

Classic landscape

The following steps and techniques are used in most classic encaustic landscapes – ironed-on sky, low hills, foliage and grasses, lakes and dotted flowers.

Requirements

- Encaustic iron or travelling iron
- Waxes – a selection of colours
- A6 card
- Stylus – optional

Ironed-on sky

1. Load the iron with the white wax first, followed by two diagonal lines of the other two colours that you have chosen for the sky; in this case, coral and pink.

2. Lay the card vertically and towards the top of your backing paper, turn the iron over and place it on the top third of the card. In one smooth action (no jerking or stopping) pull the iron towards yourself and completely off the card.

HINT: A common mistake is to lift the iron off the card before you have completed the action. This will result in a 'lifting effect', which is not what you want at this stage.

3. The sky is formed in one movement, or two, at most. If you keep going over it, it will mix completely to one colour. However, if you are not happy, you can always reload the iron and start again.

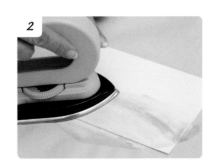

Low hills

These hills look natural in a land-scape. An important part of creating the hills is to be able to guide your iron in the right direction. So decide what colour you want for your hills and take it from there …

1. Load your iron with green wax and a small band of brown wax down the left-hand side of the base plate.

2. Begin by placing the card horizontally on the backing paper. Now place the iron under the sky – horizontally – and move it from left to right (if you are right-handed and the opposite way if you are left-handed) in a zigzag motion heading towards the bottom of your card. If the iron sticks, just release the pressure a little and carry on. Through teaching I have found that describing this movement 'like a feather falling' has been most helpful, or if that doesn't work for you, imagine doing a 'lazy figure of eight'.

Note: A common mistake is to guide your iron in the wrong direction. For example, you make a semicircle (like an 'N'), pointing the nose of the iron towards the top of your card. This results in very rounded hills with no valleys. By simply guiding the iron in a 'U' shape, you will create lovely valleys.

HINT: If you have an unsatisfactory result, simple reload you iron and start again.

1

2

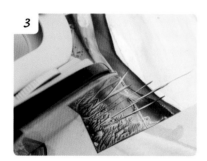

3

4

4

Foliage and grasses

This is the last stage of your landscape. You will use lifting (see techniques on page 18) to create foliage, small tufts of grass and bushes almost effortlessly. The more wax you load onto your iron, the more intense the foliage, and the less wax, the finer the foliage. Remember too, that there is already a layer of wax where your foliage will go (the bottom of your hills) so be careful not to add too much new wax to your iron when creating the foliage.

1. Dot the base of your iron with a small amount of olive green and red violet wax. Turn the iron so that the point is facing the side of your card, in other words, the straight edge of the iron is parallel to the top of the card.

2. Dab the iron quickly onto the bottom third of your card, stop and check; sometimes just one or two quick dabs of the iron creates the best foliage. The more you dab, the more the waxes mix.

3. Use the edge of your iron to create long grasses, and the point to make short tufts of grass.

4. Lastly, holding your iron like a pen, dip only the tip into pastel-coloured wax and add some summer flowers to your foreground. You can also draw these flowers in with the stylus, dipping the drawing tip into the various pastel waxes and creating a carpet of flowers. If you accidentally make a big blob, allow it to dry and simply scrape off.

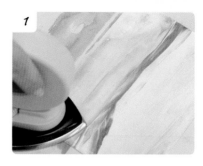

1

Lakes

You use the smoothing technique on page 18 to add a lake to your landscape. The iron leaves vertical reflections behind as you smooth it over the card. These reflections appear to have come from the sky onto your lake, giving it a very tranquil look.

1. Load the iron delicately with a lot of white and a little blue. When smoothing the colour onto your card, go into the hills to bring down into the lake what looks like their reflection in the water.

2. Once your lake is completed, create foliage, reeds and grasses as described before.

Rubbing and scratching

Requirements

- A6 card
- Waxes – a selection of colours
- Iron
- Stylus
- Tissues
- Scriber

Simple techniques such as rubbing and scratching are used extensively to add further interesting elements to basic landscapes. The stylus is used to add finishing touches such as bulrushes, birds and dragonflies.

Rubbed sky

1. Rub a small patch of blue and red violet wax onto your backing paper. Then rub your finger quickly over the wax using your body heat to slightly warm the wax. The wax pigment will be transferred onto your finger, which you then rub over the sky area. This is a very pale, soft and subtle sky, yet it is really effective. Don't just stick to the blues and pinks; experiment with your own ideas, using different coloured wax.

2. The wax can be added directly to your card by applying it like a crayon, but this creates lines, making it difficult to get a completely smooth sky. However, you can certainly practise this method if you want your rubbed sky to be a little bit darker.

HINT: Ensure that you have no sharp edges on your block of wax (they form definite lines). To do this, take the block of wax and slide it a few times over some spare paper, thereby creating an even, smooth edge. Hold the block lengthways and choose the smallest edge of the wax to smooth.

Steep hills

1. These hills are done exactly the same way as low hills, but instead of guiding your iron in a fairly low curve, angle it closer to 45 degrees, creating higher hills and deeper valleys.

2. Add foliage and grasses as explained before (see page 42).

HINT: When loading your iron with the green and brown wax, take gold wax and lay a band about 5 mm down the left side of the iron. This will highlight the tops of your hills.

Rivers

You can achieve amazing distance and depth by simply adding a river – by rubbing it into the hills while the wax is still warm, or by carefully scratching away dried wax. To be realistic your river must be scratched or rubbed parallel to the top and bottom of your card.

1. Find a beginning, and an end at a vanishing point. Usually a river begins fairly wide at the bottom of your picture and carries on up in a lazy zigzag motion, following the contours at the base of the hills. You have to be quick so you can start rubbing while the wax is still warm.

2. Roll a tissue tightly to form a point. Use this point to rub the wax off while still warm. Rub from left to right, and right to left, following the contours through the valley. Sometimes bits of wax remain; keep them, as they look like little islands in your river. Tidy up the edges

HINT: If the wax has dried and you do not manage to rub off any, place a hairdryer at the back of your picture and heat *carefully*. Then continue.

3. Alternatively, use the scriber or something similar to scrape away some wax to form a river. The wax may have stained the card so you won't get a completely white river, but the effect will be achieved nevertheless.

HINT: The hills need to be cool and dry before you can use this technique.

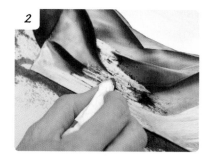

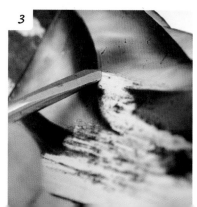

Rocks

1. Load the iron with some brown and black wax and use a smaller movement than for hills to form rocks. Use the nose of the iron to add ridges.

Bulrushes

Rivers and lakes need bulrushes.

1. Add this by loading the top edge of your iron with brown wax.

2. Place it on your landscape and form the bulrush in a small rocking motion. Add tall grasses and reeds.

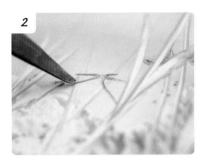

Birds and dragonflies

1. Use the stylus to form your birds. The most important thing when drawing the birds is to start from the body and flick outwards – this forms one wing. When doing the other wing, begin at the body again, flicking in the opposite direction. Be sure not to make the wings too long and repeat this to form three birds.

2. If you have water in the form of rivers or lakes, dragonflies are always a lovely addition. The best way to draw a dragonfly is to dip the drawing tip of the stylus into gold wax. Then begin by drawing one

dragonfly's top wings exactly as you would draw your birds, as described above. Now dip your tip into a little more gold and draw the bottom wings in exactly the same way. There should still be enough wax in the tip to draw the body. So place the tip in the middle of the wings and, with a flick of the stylus, draw in the body. To darken the insects, mix a little brown wax in with the gold (use the backing paper like an artist's palette). If your background is very light, it's a good idea to make them darker.

Stormy or snowy landscape

A blown sky, snow-covered peaks, low grassy hills and fir trees give different results altogether, still most pleasing and instantly achieved.

Requirements

- Iron
- Waxes – a selection of colours
- A6 card
- Hairdryer
- Stylus

Blown sky

1. Load the iron with white and a bit of black wax. The pigments are very strong, so use sparingly. Cover half of the card with this wax.

2. Use a hairdryer on a strong, hot setting hover and constantly move the hairdryer over your work to melt the wax. Once the wax has melted, the blast of air pushes it in different directions, thus creating a fantastic, dramatic sky. Stop when you are happy with the effect. Do not overwork the wax. The secret to a dramatic, stormy sky lies in knowing when to stop.

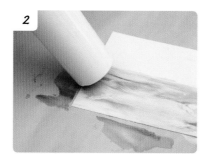

Low hills

3. Add low, grassy hills in the foreground (see page 41). I used yellow ochre and olive green and finished off my picture with foliage and blue flowers (see page 42).

Peaks

If you battle with peaks, just practise a little. You need to wait for the wax to run off the edge of the iron, which is facing *away* from you, and you use this edge to form the hills. Once you have mastered the technique, the result is really beautiful, especially when using grey for a snow scene.

4. Load the iron with the grey wax, quite near the right-hand-side of the base plate. Turn the iron onto its edge and wait for the wax to gather and move towards that edge. With the handle facing you, place the iron on the card and slowly start sliding it away from you, pushing it towards the top of the card and slowly down again. You will see the mountains and peaks start to form. Carry on until you have reached the end of your card.

5. Add depth by forming a second row of peaks if you wish. You could also take this level just halfway.

Snowy hills

6. Add low, snowy hills in the foreground, using grey and a little green, pulling down some of the grey of the snowy peaks.

Fir trees

7. Fir trees work well with a snow scene. Attach the brush tip to your stylus and use wax in various greens. Practise using the brush tip until you manage to get just the right amount of wax by dipping the hot tip into the wax. Start at the base of the tree, on the left, and take diagonal lines up, overlapping them.

8. Go back to the base and form a skirt on the right, then work from the top down with the same linear movements to complete the right of the tree.

9. Mix different greens on the brush to add shading and dimension. Reload with a lighter colour to add highlights if necessary.

10. Add more trees following the same steps.

11. Use a subtle rubbed sky (see page 43) with snowy peaks, otherwise your picture may become drab and grey.

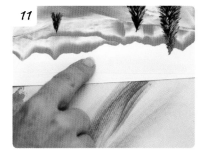

Landscape using a hot tray

You can create a stunning picture using only a hot tray and wax. If you feel like a change, use different coloured card, for example silver, bronze or gold.

Requirements

- Paper
- Pencil
- Hot tray
- Wax – black
- Bronze A5 card

1. On a piece of paper, roughly sketch your picture, keeping it simple. Turn on the hot tray and place the card onto it.

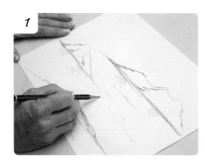

2. Using the wax to draw with, lightly copy your rough drawing. You will notice the whole card gets hot. Once you have completed the first section of your picture, lift it slightly so the heat doesn't continue melting the wax. Move your card around and try to heat only the section you are working on.

Landscape variations

Trees, fences, posts, houses and paths can all be additions to your landscape for further variations. If your landscape is a fantasy then the addition of castles with turrets and dragons can be used for variation.

Trees

Trees can be added to any land-scape. If drawn well, they can be the focus of a picture too. This is achieved by spending a lot of time adding highlights and leaf detail to the tree.

1. If you cannot draw trees, don't worry, they are not that difficult. It's a good idea to start off with an image to copy. First draw the tree lightly with a pencil and then fill it in with wax. Trees are drawn with light and dark brown waxes, using the stylus with the drawing tip attached to do so. Something that will make your trees look more realistic is to try to imagine where the light is coming from and make this the lighter side of your branches. In addition, you can use the scriber to remove the wax where the light falls on the bark, including the trunk and branches too. This gives them a rounded and three-dimensional look.

2. To add leaves to your tree, you have to change the tip of the stylus to the brush tip. Dip the brush tip into the chosen wax (for example greens and browns), and form leaves using a stippling or dabbing motion. If you find that too much wax has been soaked up in the brush, place it on a bit of tissue to remove the excess and continue placing the leaves where you want them.

Paths, posts and fences

3. For a path, find a natural route and scrape it in as you would a river (see page 44), but simulate railway sleepers.

4. Follow an imaginary line to place the posts and fences and draw them with the stylus with the drawing tip attached. The key to a realistic fence is to begin bigger in the foreground of your picture and slowly decrease the size of it the further away you go. This same rule applies if you are adding trees or a path. Eventually your fence will end at the vanishing point on your landscape. Always pay attention to the right perspective.

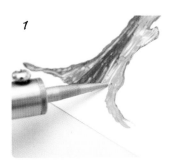

1

2

Creating flowers

Wax is a wonderful medium for creating flowers. It is translucent so forms realistic-looking petals. The technique used to draw the flowers depends on the type of project on which you are working.

1. Foxgloves are made with the tip of the iron. On a completed landscape, choose one of the long grasses to be the centre of your flower – it's a good idea to have a picture of a foxglove on hand to copy. Now turn the card upside down. (Yes, these flowers are created upside down!)

2. Load only the tip of the iron with red violet wax. Holding the iron so that only the tip touches the card, place the tip about 3 mm from the chosen grass and flick the iron towards the centre shaft at an angle until you have reached the top. Your wax application should get lighter as you go up higher. Repeat the same process on the other side of the grass shaft.

3. Take a scriber – or a knitting needle – and scratch small circles at the front of each flower to create the illusion of the flower's trumpet.

HINT: If you are doing a Mother's Day card, for example, another option is to create just the grass and flowers, leaving out the landscape background.

4. You can also create fields of small flowers by simply choosing different waxes and dabbing them straight onto the heated landscape. Dot the wax at the bottom of your hills, where it melts in small amounts, creating a sea of scattered flowers, as you often see growing wild. Don't hold the card on the iron for too long as it may distort your card. Rather heat and dab small bits of the picture at a time.

Miniature landscapes

I recently attended a miniature fair and for anyone who has never attended such a fair, it is absolutely fascinating! Anything you can imagine is made in miniature, from everything you would find in a carpenter's workshop, to knitted jerseys for miniature bears and dolls, to a full-scale miniature doll's house. It was when I was peering into this wonderland of little houses that I realized there was a place for encaustic miniature landscapes.

In one beautiful house, the lounge area had a fireplace, lounge suite, carpets and side tables; even a miniature cat sleeping in front of the fireplace! It was then that I realised how fantastic a beautiful painting would look above the fireplace.

So I went on a mission to find an ornate frame and make a picture. I bought a miniature silver tray from a craft shop and also bought genuine miniature frames at the miniature fair. Then I cut the card according to the size of the tray, using a corner punch to round the corners. I used the same landscape techniques that we have just covered, creating a tiny land-scape and working with the encaustic iron. Very little wax was needed. When completed, I sealed the picture with wax sealer and glued it to the silver tray using silicone glue.

You can create any picture in miniature using wax. I have done some other examples in the various frames bought at the fair.

The framed pictures above are hardly bigger than postage stamps and were great fun to make. I used the normal size iron for the landscapes.

Landscape on canvas

Follow the hot tray method described on page 48 for this project. The only difference is you are using a piece of loose canvas (obtainable from art and craft shops) rather than card, and various colours as you would when painting a normal landscape. One thing to remember is that this method uses slightly more wax but it does give your artwork a lovely texture. Take care not to leave the canvas too long on the hot plate as the wax may melt and run and this may distort your picture. You can use a stylus to add detail to the picture if you wish.

Inspired aloes

The landscape on the next two pages was inspired by a painting by Sally Scott. This will give you an idea of the level of painting that is possible with encaustic techniques. All it takes is a little practice.

Fantasy Landscape

This type of picture is very popular and looks great with a border around it. I like to use all the vibrant colours and try to stay away from the opaque waxes. There is no right or wrong way with fantasy pictures. What you are trying to do is to let your imagination go and see what happens. Because it's a fantasy you are allowed to have purple or green skies and blue hills or any colour you choose. In this case it's simply called 'art' and is totally acceptable!

Requirements

- Iron
- Variety of coloured waxes
- White A6 or A5 card
- Stylus
- Scriber
- Pencil
- Ruler
- Soft cloth

1. Begin by creating the hills. See landscapes on page 41.

2. Load your iron with blue and form a lake using the smoothing technique, pulling the background down for the reflection.

3. Make the foreground hills, then, using the lifting technique, create some foliage in the foreground. Add more wax to your iron if you want thick, dense foliage or just use the iron's heat to melt the existing wax if you prefer finer foliage.

4. Rub the sky as described on page 43, using shades of blue and green.

5. Use your stylus to form castles. Don't worry if you cannot draw; the castles are created by drawing straight lines next to each other, gradually going from smaller to taller, and then smaller again.

HINT: Start your lines at the bottom of the castle and finish off by lifting the stylus at the top. In this way your lines automatically go thinner at the end. Also, try to keep the lines parallel to the side of the card. Practise this on a separate piece of card until you have the hang of it.

6. Add windows to your castle by using the scriber and removing small amounts of wax up the side of the castle. Draw in, or scrape, a bridge between the two turrets.

7. For the reflection of the castles, use a soft cloth and lightly rub away some colour in the lake.

Note: If you wish, you can add a border (see page 39).

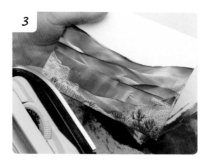

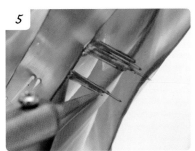

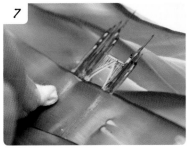

Seascape

Though this is a quick project, it is very effective. With this seascape, you will notice I have not covered the whole card – there is a lot of what I call 'white space'. This makes the picture that more dramatic, confirming the saying, "Less is more". The white space in the foreground becomes the beach and highlights in the sea.

Requirements

- Iron
- Waxes – white, blue, blugreen, turquoise, olive green, red violet, grey and black
- White A6 card
- Stylus
- Soft tissue

1. Turn the card vertically and create the sky by loading white, blue and a little grey wax onto the base of the iron. Lay the iron over the top third of the card and pull it downwards, towards yourself. Repeat this step if you are not happy with the first result. You may need to add a little more wax onto the base of the iron.

2. Wipe the iron clean and load with a little bit of olive green in the middle and then a bit of red violet dotted onto the base.

3. Dab the iron over the bottom half of your card, very quickly and lightly. The more white patches you see, the better. Don't put too much pressure on the iron, which results in parts of it not touching the entire card. As an alternative, hold the card in your hand between your thumb and index finger, using the four fingers as a springboard for the iron to lean onto. Then dab the iron lightly on the bottom half of your card to create the grasses and bushes on your beach. Load more

and repeat if you are not happy with the first run.

4. Take light blue, bluegreen or turquoise wax and horizontally colour the sea area. This is a rough texture and you will see it is quite different from the effect you get when you place the wax on with the iron. If you want to blend the sea area a bit more, rub over it with your finger.

5. Buff the picture with a soft tissue and finish it by drawing in a couple of birds, using the stylus and black wax. The reason you buff before adding finer details is because they might smudge when you rub over them because of the light sky behind.

Underwater fantasy

The colours used in this project are effective as they are vivid and translucent. *Fantasy* means just that … you can create a scene using unusual colours and fantasy castles.

Requirements

- Iron
- Blue, purple and fluorescent pink waxes
- White A6 or A5 card
- Stylus (optional)
- Scriber

1. Load the base of the iron with small amounts of blue and pink wax. Turn the iron over and cover the card with the smoothing technique. It's not too important if the whole card is not completely covered, because we are going to work different parts of the card and eventually, it will all be developed into part of the picture.

2. Add purple and use the lifting technique to form banks of coral all round, then add some rocks.

3. When doing the background, you may notice air gaps develop under the iron, forming 'castles' without any deliberate effort from you – that's the magic of encaustic! Now use your scriber or stylus to develop these castles further and give them more definition if they are not too clear. If you have a stylus, draw in the castles by dipping the hot drawing tip into one of your darker shades of wax – perhaps the purple and draw in the turrets of your castles. If you haven't managed to form any natural castles, or you don't have a stylus, use the scriber to create them by scratching lines to form the turrets.

4. Enhance the foliage with the scriber if you wish.

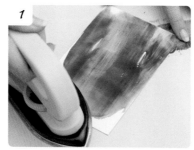

5. Look for other creatures like jellyfish that may have formed, and enhance them with the scriber. Add bubbles using the scriber.

6. Create kelp using only the edge of your iron, sliding it up towards the top of the card, swaying the iron from left to right – a ribbon-effect should form. You will only need a few of these, as your picture is already quite busy.

7. If you wish, add a simple border (see page 39).

HINT: The veining effect, which is so characteristic of encaustic art, is achieved by lifting the iron off the card. When forming an underwater scene, this veining effect mimics the coral, creating a very realistic scene.

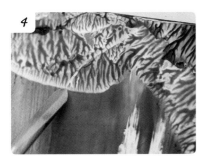

4

6

7

Celebration cards and embellishments

It seems that nowadays everyone simply uses the computer or a cellphone to send wishes for birthdays and other occasions. There is nothing nicer than receiving a handmade card from a close friend or family member for that special occasion – use these ideas to get back into this tradition.

There are many different ways to create Christmas cards using encaustic. You can use any Christmas-themed stamps and make wonderful cards incorporating

traditional Christmas colours or the colours of the season. If you have a lot of cards to make, using stamps speeds up the process, but once in a while it's fun to create a card entirely with wax and a bit of imagination.

Thankyou cards, birthday cards, Mother's and Father's Day cards are further examples of cards you can create using encaustic techniques. Often your card is so beautiful and special that the recipient may want to frame it, turning the card itself into a lasting gift.

Christmas snow scene

The following example is one I have done using blues and purples. One thing to remember here is that your picture is made up of layers; the background is done first and the window frame next. Then add the fir trees and log cabin, followed by the snow, and buff.

Requirements

- Iron
- Pastel blue wax
- Purple, brown, silver and white waxes
- White A6 card
- Stylus
- Pencil
- Tissue

1. Create the sky by loading your iron with a small amount of pastel blue and purple and a little white. Turn your card vertically, and cover one third of it by laying the iron over it and, in a smooth motion, pulling the iron towards yourself.

2. Turn the card horizontally and create the snowy hills by loading your iron with a little purple wax and using the smoothing technique.

3. Load the iron with a strip of dark purple on one side of the base plate; slide it down the edge of the top half of the card, and down the edge of the bottom half to form curtains. Turn the card upside down to do the other side. Draw the tiebacks with your stylus and silver wax.

4. Draw the window panes using a pencil; dip your stylus into the brown wax to go over the pencil lines.

5. Create the fir trees in pastel blue, dipping the stylus into these colours and drawing in the trees. I simply used dots applied in lines, going from bigger to smaller as I worked up the tree – a simple, yet effective way of doing small trees.

6. Use the stylus for the log cabin and scrape away some wax to suggest snow. Add snowflakes in either a dark or light colour.

Christmas camels

This lovely Christmas card is done using a stamp and then filling in the background over the stamp. Solid stamps work best when used in combination with encaustic art.

1. Begin by stamping the three wise men stamp onto the middle of your card.

2. Melt a small amount of golden yellow and white onto the base of the iron and lay this wax onto the bottom half of the card, using the smoothing method. If you want a shade a little closer to the colour of sand, add a small amount of brown and yellow ochre. Ensure that the camels look as if they are on the ground by placing the horizon right at their feet.

3. The long shadows drawn in front of the camels in golden yellow turn this Christmas card into something special. They are not hard to do; just copy mine and you will see how easy they are. Use the stylus to do this, but pencil first if you don't feel confident that you can do it.

4. Dip your stylus into the gold wax and make the big star, then add small dots in gold and golden yellow to form stars.

Requirements

- Three wise men Christmas stamp
- Permanent inkpad
- White A6 card
- Golden yellow, brown, yellow ochre, gold and white waxes
- Iron
- Scriber
- Fine-tipped permanent marker
- Stylus
- Tissue
- Wax sealer
- Peel-offs

5. Buff your picture with a soft tissue or cloth and coat with wax sealer.

6. Add Christmas wording using peel-offs or write it in a permanent marker if you have a good handwriting.

3

4

4

Wax-stamped Christmas card

Gold or silver wax stamped onto dark background or black wax on gold or silver creates a stunning but simple image for Christmas or other celebration cards, giving instant results. You will be using two pieces of card – one to act as a stamping pad, and the other to stamp onto. This technique will also work well on a hot tray.

Requirements

- Iron
- White A6 card
- Coloured A5 card
- Black wax
- Red chord
- Rubber stamp of Christmas bauble

1. Assemble the iron as a mini-hot plate.

2. Place the card onto the hot plate and load some black wax onto the card – this acts as a palette. Do not use too much wax as this could lead to a smudged print. Practise on a piece of scrap paper before stamping onto your card.

3. Whilst the palette is still on the base of the iron, dab the stamp into this wax to load it. Set your palette card aside and place the coloured card onto the iron. Stamp the image, taking care not to slip or slide! Lift it off.

4. Continue stamping until your composition is complete. This card surface is very forgiving so you can "clean up" any unwanted wax by taking some tissue and rubbing it off carefully.

5. Finish off your card by attaching a length of red chord to each Christmas bauble. Attach this picture to another folded greeting card and write your special message inside.

Note: To clean the stamp, dab it onto the hot iron and press onto tissue or backing paper. Repeat until all the wax has been removed.

2

3

3

Heart Valentine's card

Embossing is used by many card enthusiasts. To create this card, you simply add wax to the background. You can use one colour, as I have done here, or several colours. The Christmas holly (below) was created by embossing; when the green wax was dry, I removed the wax from the berry area with my scriber and added red using the stylus.

Requirements

- Iron
- White A6 card
- Scriber or knitting needle
- Soft working surface
- Wax in your colour of choice
- Tissue

1. Place the card, right side up, on a surface such as a face cloth, duster or old magazine, soft enough to ensure you will get a deep imprint.

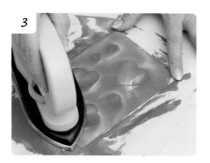

2. Draw a freehand design with the scriber or knitting needle. Press hard enough to get a good imprint, but not too hard as you may tear the card.

3. Load your iron with colour and apply a thin layer to the card. The wax floods into the groves created on the card, leaving dark and light shades on the different surface levels. Finish with embellishments and place in a window card.

HINT: This technique is suitable for any theme imaginable.

Father's Day card or scrapbooking addition

There always seem to be so many more ideas for the ladies but not too many for men. However, sport is usually a good idea for a man's card, so I am going to show you how to do a simple Father's Day card with a golf theme. This could also be used on a scrapbook page.

Requirements

- Iron
- White A6 card
- Blue, white, leaf green, green, brown, red and black waxes
- Scriber
- Ruler
- Tissue
- Glue
- Embellishments
- Small white pompon
- Father's Day peel-off sticker

1. Begin by creating a sky, referring to any of the previous examples on how to create a sky. I have used blue and white but you can change these colours if you so choose.

2. Create a golf green. Load your iron with leaf green and green wax and smooth the wax evenly across your card in one movement, like you would do for a lake.

3. Take the scriber and make the 'hole' by scratching a small circle in the green part of your picture.

4. Use a ruler to scrape away a line of wax where the flagpole will go. Dip the stylus into the brown wax and draw in the pole.

5. Scrape away the wax where the flag will go, then use the red wax to draw in the flag.

Note: You remove the wax to achieve a true brown and a true red. If you don't do this, the heat from the stylus will melt the green underneath. So if you want the true colour you are working with, and there is already wax on the card, simply remove it and continue in the chosen colour.

6. Shine your picture with a soft tissue and draw the birds with the stylus, using black wax, as described on page 45.

7. Place your picture in a framed card. Attach the embellishments. Finish off by placing a Father's Day sticker at the top of the card if you wish.

4

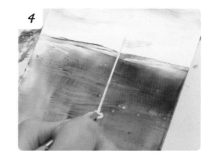

1

2

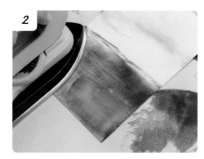

6

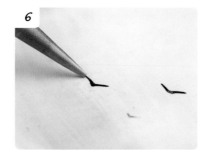

Mother's Day card

I used a butterfly theme for my card. The challenge when doing butterflies is symmetry. As you know, butterflies have mirror image wings so this technique is perfect to create that effect. I used peel-off stickers for the wording.

Requirements

- White A6 card
- Bone folder
- Iron
- Brightly coloured waxes
- Butterfly stencil or template (see page 126)
- Stylus
- Scriber or pencil
- Wax sealer
- Scissors
- Clear glue
- Rhinestones
- Glass-paint liner (optional)
- Contrasting card to mount butterfly

1. Fold the card in half and rub the bone folder over the fold to flatten it without marking the card. You can also use the plastic handle of a pair of scissors but if you are going to be making a lot of cards, a bone folder is a good investment.

2. Open up the card and lay a couple of bright colours onto *one* side of the card until it is covered in wax. Do not use too much wax.

3. Fold the card so that the un-waxed side sits on top of the waxed side. Iron over the card, holding it there for a few seconds so the heat penetrates through it, melting the wax on the other side. Work right into the fold. At this point, you may have to turn the heat up a little on your iron. While still warm, open up your card and let it cool.

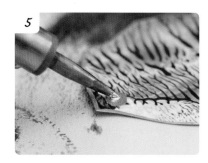

Happy Mothers Day

4. Place the butterfly stencil over the waxed area, with the body centred on the fold and trace around it with a pencil or scriber. Cut it out. If you have a stylus you can add further detail by drawing in dots and typical butterfly markings onto the wings or alternatively use the scriber to form delicate circles and shapes. Work carefully, as the wax damages easily before it is coated.

3

6

5. Using the stylus, outline it with silver wax, lifting it up to ensure the wax does not mix with the colours. Add more detail to the wings using silver wax, keeping in mind that the wings must be a morror image. Edge the feelers in silver and black and fill in the body in black.

6. Buff the butterfly, coat it with a layer of wax sealer and bend the wings slightly. Enhance the image by adding rhinestones. When dry, apply glue to the body of the

butterfly only and stick it onto the plain card.

HINT: To add a little more detail, use the iron to create a border around the card before adhering the butterfly (see borders on page 39).

7. Assemble the card and add the wording.

73

Funky fish card

One day I took out my iron and began a picture in the usual way (which is basically not really knowing what I want to do). I placed the iron flat on one half of the card and then smoothed it off. To my amazement, a fish appeared out of nowhere … and this is how my picture was born.

Requirements

- White A6 card
- Iron
- Bright purple, red-violet, lime green, olive green, gold and brown wax
- Stylus
- Scriber
- Backing card

1. Load half of the base of the iron with some bright purple and a touch of red violet wax. Place the iron on the top righthand side of the card and move it in the form of a back-to-front C to form the mouth of the fish. In one movement, come back up about 5 mm closer to the edge, almost to the starting point, and slide down, curving first left, then right.

2. To create the second fish, turn your card around and do exactly the same, using the lime green wax.

3. Hold the iron at a 45° angle and use the tip to create the scales. With this technique you are removing the wax, revealing the white card underneath.

4. Dab a small amount of brown and red violet wax in the middle of the iron and form your coral using the lifting effect. Add a few rocks by smoothing over.

5. Load the edge of the iron with olive green wax and wiggle the iron up the card to form kelp or sea grass.

6. Use the stylus to create the bubbles, thin grass and eyes of the fish (scratch off the wax before doing the eyes). Load some gold wax to the tip of the stylus and highlight the scales by drawing over some.

7. Buff and mount the final picture onto backing card.

Note: Refer to different ways of holding the iron for drawing, on page 8.

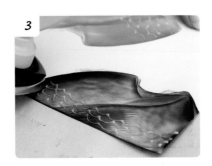

Grape celebration card

While wondering what to do after I had attached the round tip to my stylus, I came up with the idea of a bunch of grapes. The design turned out really well and I decided to use it as a theme for a scrapbook page as it would go with some pictures I took on a recent visit to a wine farm. You can use it as a design for an occasion card or take it to be framed – fruit pictures tend to look good in most kitchens.

Requirements

- Stylus
- Round tip for stylus
- Violet, red-violet, bright green and brown waxes
- White A5 card
- Drawing tip for the stylus
- Dimensional gel (available at most scrapbooking shops) or
- Wax sealer
- Scissors
- Glue

1. Form the bunch of grapes from the top to the bottom. Pencil it first if you are not confident. Attach the round tip to the stylus and turn it on. Dip the tip into the violet wax and press it onto the card. You want smooth grapes, so slide the round tip off the card. Begin each new grape over the smudge mark.

2. When you reach the last row of grapes, you will have no option but to lift the round tip off the card, so these ones will have a rough edge. Wiggle the tip in circles to remove most of the lifting effect.

3. When the stylus has cooled, replace the round tip with the drawing tip to do the leaves. Pencil first if you are not confident. Using the green and brown waxes, draw the leaves and swirls typically found on a grape vine. Dilute the colours with clear wax to fill in and shade the leaves.

4. Cover the individual grapes with a thin layer of dimensional gel to give them a rounded effect, leaving gaps in between to define the space between the grapes. When dry, repeat this step to add even more dimension. If you don't have this product, seal your completed picture with a layer of wax sealer.

5. Mount the picture on a suitable backing and use as an occasion card.

3

3

4

1

2

Children's birthday card

This is a really simple and quick picture to make using very brightly coloured circles to form the balloons. It makes a lovely children's birthday card.

Requirements

- Iron
- Various brightly coloured waxes
- White A5 card
- Stylus
- Round tip for the stylus
- Drawing tip for the stylus
- Scriber or sharp object for scratching off wax
- Dimensional gel (available at scrapbooking shops) or
- Wax sealer
- Bows
- Glue

1. Create a background for your picture, using the iron and the smoothing effect.

2. Create the balloons by loading the round tip with indigo wax and rotating the stylus in small circles until your design resembles the shape and size of a balloon.

3. Draw in the strings that are attached to the balloons with the edge of the round tip.

4. Use the scriber or sharp tool to scratch away a little of the wax on each balloon to highlight it. This adds to the effect of making it look round and three-dimensional. Finish off with either dimensional gel or wax sealer.

5. Because the balloons are simple, make a border around the card using a contrasting colour. You can leave it plain or add detail by placing the round tip flat on the edge of the card and sliding it off, repeating this motion all the way around the border. Do a couple of layers if you wish, reloading the round tip with extra wax if needed. You now have a very pretty effect that matches your balloons.

6. Glue ribbon bows along the string to add interest and dimension.

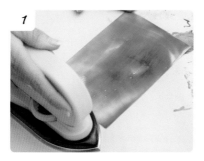

Flowers – using a palette knife

Not everyone has a palette knife handy, but if you happen to have a small one, try this method – it's quite easy and makes a lovely greeting card.

Requirements

- Hot plate assembled iron
- Waxes in three different colours: yellow, orange, red and brown
- White A6 card
- Tissue or cloth

1. Melt a little red and yellow wax onto the base of the iron. Place the palette knife flat side down into the wax, holding it there for a second or two in order to heat up the knife. Place the loaded palette knife onto your card with either the tip (narrow) or the foot (wide) in the centre of the flower and press wax on. Repeat if necessary to tidy up individual petals. Alternate the position of the palette knife between the flowers.

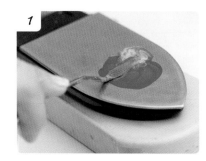

2. Continue to reload the knife after completing each petal. When your yellow flower is complete, work on the remaining flowers, using one colour at a time.

3. Melt a little brown wax on the iron and fill in the centres of the flowers by dabbing on the wax with the tip of the palette knife.

4. Leave the background plain white, or rub your finger onto one of the waxes used for your flowers, then over the area between the flowers to create a soft, subtle hint of colour. Finally, shine your picture with a soft cloth or tissue.

Dabbed-flower card

This card is really quick and easy with the flowers dabbed on. You can leave the background plain white, or add a rubbed sky.

Requirements

- Iron
- Olive green, red violet, yellow and orange waxes
- White A6 card
- Tissue or cloth

1. Load the iron with olive green and red violet wax and lay the foundation of your picture by using the lifting technique. Do not overwork this.

2. Assemble your iron in the hot plate position as shown on page 8 and place the card on it and dab on colours until you are satisfied with the result (see page 50).

3. Leave the sky plain or add a rubbed sky, buff and mount the picture.

Flowers using the micro-iron tip

The micro-iron tip is shaped like a petal, and can be used to create beautiful flowers. Manoeuvring the angle enables you to draw from very tiny to bigger flowers as well as stems and leaves. Mount your finished picture.

Requirements

- Stylus with micro-iron tip
- Various brightly coloured and green waxes
- White A 6 card
- A5 card

1. Start by deciding where to place your flowers. Try to imagine a bunch of flowers and mix the small ones with the big ones. If it helps, draw a light pencil mark to show you where the flowers are to be placed.

2. Attach the micro-iron tip to your stylus. If you hold the attachment so the sharp tip just touches the card you will have very tiny flowers. The next size flower is done by lowering the angle of the tip slightly. When doing the bigger ones the tip is

nearly flat on the card. The one half of the petal is created by drawing a C and the other half of the petal is a back-to-front C.

3. For multi-layered flowers like a dahlia, do the outside layer of petals first and work towards the centre.

4. Dab brown wax with the tip of the micro-iron to form the centre.

5. Clean the tip and draw in the stems by sliding the edge of the tip

through some olive green wax and placing it where you want your stem. The leaves are simply a flick outwards of the inside edge, scooping off rather than lifting. Just practise a bit as it is easier to do than to describe how to do it.

4

5

2

3

3

2

5

Blown flower card

These abstract flowers tend to become very 'spidery' because it's fairly difficult to control the blast of hot air from the hairdryer's nozzle. You also need a good imagination to decide where the actual flowers could be formed. Having said all this, these flowers are really fun to do, so don't be put off. This makes a really special card – a gift in its own right.

Requirements

- Iron
- White A5 card – use bright waxes *or*
- Black A5 card – use pastel waxes
- Hairdryer
- Stylus or scriber (optional)

When using the hairdryer start on the low speed and heat setting first, then put it up to the next notch. Rather don't use a paint stripper or heat gun; the paint stripper gets too hot, scorches the paper and burns the wax and, though I have used my heat gun, it also gets a bit too hot. Special heat guns for this art can be purchased but they are quite expensive.

1. Hold the hot iron at a 90° angle to the card. Now, hold the blocks of different coloured wax at the tip of the iron, letting the melted wax slide off it, creating small blobs of raised wax. Let these blobs drop here and there on the card.

2. Set the hairdryer to low speed/ heat and allow it to hover over the dots of wax, one at a time. Once you see the wax become shiny and begin to melt, set the hairdryer to high speed and heat. This is when the fun really starts, as you must remember to keep the hairdryer moving in circular movements whilst pointing in towards the inside of the dot of wax. If the wax runs all over the place, just redirect the blast of air towards the middle of your card. I sometimes find it easier to hold the card in my hand, moving the card instead of the hairdryer, so use the method that works best for you.

3. Stop the hairdryer occasionally to focus and see where the flowers are developing. Once all the dots of wax are melted, and you have some flowers formed, hold the hairdryer close to the middle of the flower for a second or two to form a beautiful centre. If you would like to cover the whole card with flowers, repeat the above stages, filling in the gaps with more dots of wax and melting and blowing the flowers until the entire card has been covered.

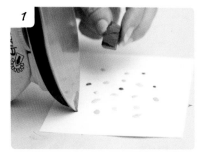

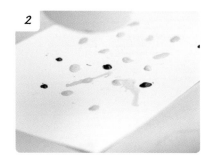

2

4. If you have a stylus, you may draw in the stamens with a small dab of either green or brown wax. If not, you can scrape the stamens with the scriber, a toothpick or use the nose of the iron. If you have used a dark card as a background and your blown flowers are in pastel colours, you can create your stamens by using the scriber and scraping away the wax to reveal the dark card underneath.

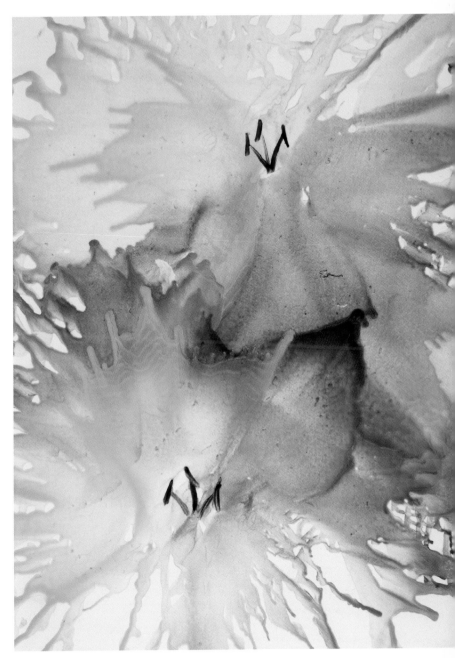

3

3

4

stamped landscape card

Rubber stamps work very well with encaustic, especially if you find it difficult to draw. You can stamp the picture directly onto your card with a permanent, fast-drying solvent ink. This aloe stamp makes a lovely focal point for a landscape and stands out beautifully filled in with bright colours. The background is added once the stamped image has dried.

Requirements

- Iron
- Stylus
- Waxes in various colours
- White A5 card
- Aloe stamp and permanent black ink stamping pad
- Scriber
- Mounting card

1. Using the ink stamp, stamp two images of the aloe in the bottom half of your card and leave to dry.

2. Load the iron with the colours you want your sky to be and apply, using the smoothing effect.

3. Complete your landscape in the appropriate colours by creating the hills using the smoothing effect, and the foreground foliage using the lifting effect (see steps under landscapes page 42).

4. Using the scriber, carefully scrape the wax off the entire aloe image to reveal the white card underneath.

5. Load the stylus with one colour at a time and fill in the white areas of the stamped image. Use clear wax between adjacent colours to ensure good blending.

Note: The reason you scrape the wax off the stamped image is that you do not want to mix the original coat of wax with the bright colours of the aloe. To keep them bright, these colours must be applied to a white base.

6. Place the completed picture onto a framed or plain card.

Stamped underwater scene with texture

- Stamp
- Permanent ink stamping pad
- White A6 card
- Iron
- Various waxes in shades of blue
- White wax
- Scriber
- Stylus
- Tissue

When solid stamps are combined with encaustic, the picture is built up around the image, depending on the type of stamp used. Because the veining effect is so characteristic of encaustic, coral is a beautiful addition to this underwater scene. Strips of single-layer tissue forming some three-dimensional underwater coral and grasses add texture and interest.

1. Stamp the image onto the card using your selected stamp and the permanent ink pad. Allow to dry.

2. Lay the wax on the base of the iron and cover the card in shades of blue using the smoothing effect.

3. Load the iron with a small amount of wax and create coral and kelp.

4. Tear small strips of single layer tissue. Attach the strips to the card using the stylus or the edge of the iron and small amounts of wax in the same colour. Leave the fringy sides free and only attach the centre vein to the card. Now add different shades of light coloured wax to the tissue.

5. Develop the picture by adding bubbles, either with the stylus or by scraping away the wax with the scriber. Dip the stylus tip into the white wax and draw in the eyes.

6. The stamped image will have a thin coat of wax covering it. Remove this wax with a scriber leaving a 1 mm border on one side of the stamp. This will give the image definition.

7. Place the finished picture into a framed or plain card.

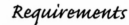

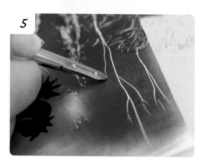

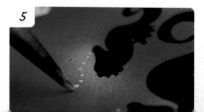

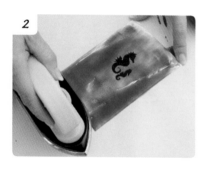

Silhouettes on encaustic background

Requirements

- Design
- Transfer paper
- Permanent black ink marker
- White A5 card
- Wax in suitable colours
- Iron
- Scriber

Solid images on a background created wth encaustic techniques also make for a pleasing, interesting effect. You can either cut the sihouette images from black card or hand-draw them. The templates are on page 127.

1. Trace a silhouette image onto the white card. I used a photograph taken by my good friend Karen Tunley in Springbok in the North-ern Cape, South Africa. This is a demonstration of how to interpret a photograph and recreate it in your own style.

2. Draw and colour in with the black permanent marker and allow to dry.

3. Lay your background over the silhouette, working it until you are happy with the result.

4. To remove the layer of wax covering the drawn image, use the scriber, taking care not to scratch the card. If you do scrape away some of the permanent marker, simply fill it in again.

Note: You can also cut out a silhouette from black card and attach it using small squares of double-sided tape. If you have chosen a bird, water makes a lovely background. If you choose an animal, a landscape with hills and valleys is good. When you have completed the background, remove the backing off your double-sided tape and position your silhouette onto the picture.

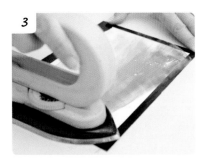

Waxed serviette card

Serviettes come in a range of lovely prints and using a printed serviette is an easy way to make a card because it already has a design. The picture is enhanced by adding a layer of clear wax, giving a lovely finish and adhering it to the backing card at the same time. Once the wax has dried, you can further enhance sections of the printed image by adding more colour, using the stylus.

Requirements

- Printed serviette
- White square backing card
- Scissors
- Stylus
- Clear or candle wax to attach the seviette (plus additional colours if you need them)
- Stylus with micro-iron attachment
- Window card

1. Begin by cutting out the section of the serviette you have chosen. Keep the layers together if possible, as this makes cutting easier. Separate and use the top layer only. Position the serviette picture where you want it.

2. Load your iron with clear or candle wax and iron onto the serviette. (Beeswax adds a lovely sheen.) Keep the iron on the serviette to avoid getting wax onto the backing card. Because the wax is an adhesive, it sticks or attaches the serviette to the card.

3. My picture needed some definition so I used the stylus and various waxes in colours matching that of the design to outline, colour in or otherwise enhance the overall look of my picture.

4. Place the completed encaustic work into a window card or attach to plain card.

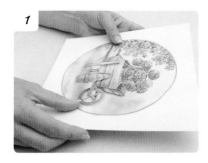

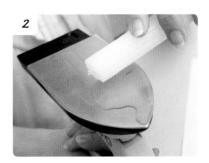

Vellum decals

Peel-off stickers are versatile and can look really professional on a project. I used them on vellum to make decals, adding lovely translucent colour with wax. Use them on glass doors or windows as a decoration or do some in a Christmas theme for the season.

Requirements

- Peel-off stickers
- Vellum
- Stylus
- Various coloured waxes
- Double-sided tape
- Backing card

1. Carefully position the sticker onto the vellum and smooth it down thoroughly.

2. Dip the stylus into the various coloured waxes, using them to fill in the gaps on the sticker.

3. Cut out the completed picture, place a small piece of double-sided tape onto the back and stick it onto a window or sliding door. Alternatively, mount it and use as a Christmas card.

HINT: These decals will also make a lovely mobile if strung up. The wax finish on the sheer vellum creates a lovely see-through effect.

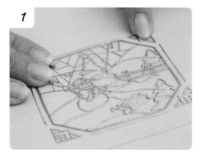

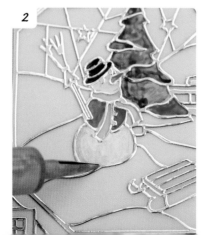

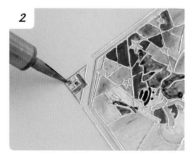

Concertina mini picture screen

Use aperture cards or make your own, joining them to form a concertina card, inserting different encaustic pictures. The screen makes a very nice present as well as an unusual card and is great for showing off this craft.

Requirements

- 4 small encaustic pictures half A6 size (always keep your discards as a small section may be just right)
- Wax sealer
- Clear glue
- 4 aperture cards – I used size 740 mm x 105 mm
- Peel-offs

1. Seal your four small pictures with wax sealer. Glue each of these, one by one, into an aperture card.

2. To cover the backs of the pictures that can be seen trough the aperture cards, glue the solid part of the second card over the back of the first card. Continue until you have covered all four rough backs.

3. Add peel-offs to enhance the screen or convey a greeting.

Encaustic mosaics card

Requirements

- Encaustic picture
- Square punch
- Pencil
- Scissors
- Backing card – any colour
- Clear glue
- Card for mounting the picture
- Dimensional gel – available from most scrapbooking shops

Encaustic mosaics are such fun to make. You can mosaic a picture you have made especially for this purpose, or take this as the perfect opportunity to use up those pictures that didn't seem 'quite right'.

1. Use the square punch to cut out the entire picture. Try to punch out the squares right next to each other, as this keeps the picture even.

2. As you punch out a square, number it on the back with a pencil.

3. Stamp in rows up, then cut away the remaining frame before punching the next row.

4. Place the squares onto the backing card, and see if you need to trim it before you start sticking the squares onto this card. If so, do it now. Put a small amount of glue on the back of the square and place it onto the card. Carry on until you have laid all your mosaic tiles in numerical order.

5. Once they have dried, follow the manufacturer's instructions for applying the dimensional gel, taking care not to get the gel on your backing card. Leave this to dry for three to four hours and repeat. Your tiles will now look like glazed, ceramic tiles.

Note: You can also place the tiles randomly to create a completely different effect. This may be a good way to use an encaustic picture where you felt the colours or composition did not work as this will change altogether.

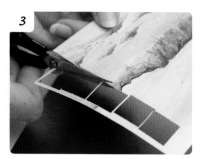

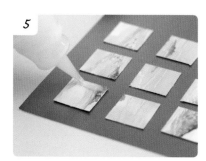

Encaustic mosaics embellishment

I used discarded pictures that didn't really turn out that well for these frames. Once the tiles have been punched it is easy to combine them in a visually pleasing pattern.

Requirements

- Encaustic pictures
- Square punch
- Scissors
- Backing card or frame
- Clear glue
- Dimensional gel

HINT: Keep all your unwanted work; it may just come in handy for projects such as this.

1. You don't have to be careful with precise punching on this project because you are not putting together a picture. So look for interesting parts of the picture and punch away, collecting colours that complement each other.

2. These tiles can be used in many ways. Embellish a scrapbooking page; add them to a painted, wooden blank to create a 'real' mosaic effect, or simply use as a border on an occasion card or frame.

3. Apply dimensional gel and leave to dry. The tiles are quite handy to keep on standby for that urgent card or gift.

HINT: If you are going to handle your stamped tiles a lot, for example, gluing them to a tin or to a wooden object, I would advise that you glue them first and then coat carefully, trying not to get the dimensional gel on the background. Unfortunately, sometimes the gel comes away if the tile is bumped, buckled or handled a lot, so take care.

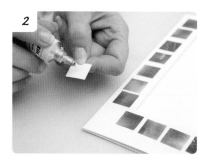

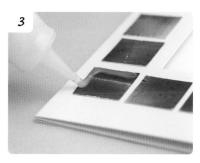

Pastel flowers on black card

These flowers with their whispy, ethereal look are not all that difficult to create and a card like this will be treasured and most likely find its way into a permanent frame.

Requirements

- Black A5 card
- Pastel blue, white and blue transparent wax
- Iron
- Scriber
- Soft cloth

1. Load the iron with blue, white and pastel blue wax.

2. Start in the middle and lay the wax down in scoops to the right. Work with the half of the iron closest to you and go round in a circle.

3. With the edge of the iron and a little bit of pastel blue, make squiggles down the middle. Let the wax run down the back of the iron. Repeat with white.

4. Clean up bits that you don't want to tidy up the edges by rubbing off the wax with a soft cloth.

5. Buff the picture with a soft cloth and use the scriber to scratch out stamens and a black centre to ground them.

Decorative encaustic

Wax adheres to a number of surfaces, which makes it a very versatile medium. To demonstrate the versatility of encaustic art, I adapted the encaustic techniques for use on various different objects or supports. It does not matter if the item being used is a flat or curved, rough or smooth surface. Just bear in mind, if the surface is not flat the stylus is a better option of tool to use than the iron. These projects make lovely gifts.

Decorated gift boxes

These decorated gift boxes are wonderful for presenting that special small gift. They are quick and easy to make – use a template from the Internet, or buy a ready-made, pre-cut box that you fold and decorate. The pre-cut boxes are great as they have all the score lines, so it's just a matter of folding and sticking it together. (Some don't even need sticking; they just fold together.)

Requirements

- Pre-cut box
- Various coloured waxes
- Iron
- Sciber (optional)
- Stylus (optional)
- Embellishments
- Wax sealer and brush
- Clear glue

1. Using any colours and the abstract technique, load your iron with the wax and begin to cover the entire box. Note that it is not made up yet – and remember to use colours that look good together, or single colour groups. Cover all the little bits as you will see them.

2. Once the box is covered in wax, scratch out motifs, initials or names if you wish. Leave them white, or add colour with the stylus. I used silver for the heart.

3. The box needs a protective coating on it as it will be handled a lot, so buff and then apply wax sealer and leave to dry.

4. Fold the box. Glue it if necessary but try not to get glue on the design as it may lift the wax off. However, should this happen, simply dab it with the iron again to cover up the bald patch.

5. Add further embellishments such as a gold foil effect or skeleton leaves if you prefer.

All that is left is to put that special little gift, wrapped in tissue paper, into your box.

HINT: Make a few of these boxes at a time to keep on hand for last-minute gifts.

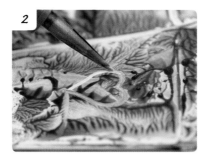

Trinket tins

Encaustic pictures can be applied in many ways to create innovative gifts. For this project I used an abstract finish on sheets of vellum to cover a set of trinket tins obtainable from good craft shops (you could also use empty food tins). The vellum is lovely and pliable, making an easy cover for the tins.

Requirements

- Round tins in various heights
- Metal primer spray paint
- White spray paint
- White and purple wax
- Vellum (pink)
- Clear adhesive glue
- Iron
- Stylus with round tip
- Sealer
- Ribbon

1. Spray-paint the tins, inside and out, with metal primer and white spray paint, allowing them to dry completely between applications, and set aside to dry.

2. Cut the vellum to fit the tins allowing a small overlap. I used pink vellum. (You can also decorate the vellum first and then cut to size, whichever you find easier.)

3. Load the iron with purple wax and smooth over the vellum.

4. Place the stylus with the round tip onto the wax background and make bubbles randomly by taking the wax off. These bubbles will appear more transparent on the purple background with some of the pink vellum shining through.

5. Change the tip to the drawing tip and highlight the bubbles with a small line of white wax.

6. Draw dots around the bubbles using the stylus and white wax.

7. Decorate a contrasting cover for some of the tins by adding circles in purple wax onto clear pink vellum. Add the highlights, then fill in the background with small white and purple dots.

8. Shine and seal the vellum, then cut to size to fit the various tins if you had not done so before you started. Glue onto the tins.

9. Measure the ribbon for each tin, cut and glue it to the top using clear glue.

Encaustic art on ostrich eggs

The idea of painting onto an ostrich egg was purely experimental, as it had never occurred to me before, but the result was really amazing. It worked very well because the egg is strong and can take heat. The pitted marks of the egg make for an unusual texture.

Requirements

- Ostrich egg
- Various brightly coloured waxes
- Hairdryer
- Design
- Pencil
- Tissue or soft cloth
- Stylus
- Polyurethane, heat-resistant hard varnish (used in decoupage and referred to as PU varnish) and brush
- Wooden bracelet used to support the completed egg

1. Choose a fairly light-coloured wax as your background. Heat the area of the egg on which you are working using the hairdryer. While still warm, take the wax block and rub it over this area, leaving patches of wax. Rub with your finger then buff lightly not to remove but to blend the colour. The pigment stays behind, staining the egg. If you have rubbed off too much, repeat this process. You will notice some of the wax actually fills the tiny holes on the surface of the egg. Let the egg cool down completely.

2. Trace your design onto tracing paper and then onto the egg. I have chosen flowers, but you can use any simple design. If you feel confident enough, draw straight onto the ostrich egg with your stylus.

3. Using the stylus, dip the drawing point into the wax and begin drawing the picture. I started at the bottom and worked my way around the bulge of the egg. The big advantage here is that the wax dries immediately, so you can continue around the egg without smudging the wax or having to wait for it to dry.

4. Repeat the same design, or use a different design on the other side of the ostrich egg. I used three different designs on my egg .

5. Once the design is completed, cover the egg with the hard varnish. This will yellow slightly with age but doesn't really matter, as the egg is already a yellowish colour.

HINT: If you prefer, you can coat your egg with a pure water-based varnish. These are often more popular with crafters as they do not discolour – and the brushes are easier to clean – though they are not quite as hzrd.

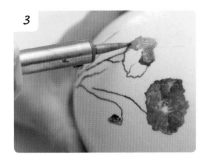

Decorating ceramics

Painting onto ceramics with wax is fairly easy – use your stylus for the best effect. Mistakes are not easily corrected, so try to be careful and accurate. Should something go wrong, rub the wax off with very fine sandpaper. The wax will smudge, but just keep sanding until all of it is gone. You can use any item, from bisque pottery sea shells to big fruit bowls. Just remember that bigger items are harder to paint, so start small.

Requirements

- Bisque pottery item
- Sponge or cloth
- Pencil
- Stylus
- Black and white waxes
- Clear candle wax
- Soft cloth

1. Wipe the item with a damp sponge. Make sure it is completely dry and free of dust before you begin decorating it. Pencil-draw your design onto the bisque ware.

2. Dip the drawing tip into the black wax and begin drawing your design. When completed, dip the tip by into some candle wax and wipe it clean with a soft cloth or kitchen towel.

3. Dip the stylus into the white wax now and draw in the spots. Don't hold the tip too long on the black wax because this will melt it and the spots might end up grey.

4. There is no need to varnish this item – I think it looks better with a matt finish to match the bisque background. If you want to, you could varnish only the birds.

Candle carving

Designing your own candles is so much fun. They are inexpensive and there are so many shapes and sizes to choose from. As your base is a clear wax (the actual candle), whatever colour wax you use for designs on it will be somewhat diluted. Therefore an important thing to remember is not to hold the stylus onto your candle for too long, but to rather use quick movements.

1. Copy or draw your design onto a piece of paper, then lightly draw the design onto the candle using a pencil or laundry marker.

If you feel confident, you can do your design free-hand with the stylus. Squiggles and scrolls work best.

2. Turn the stylus on. When hot, dip the drawing tip into the coloured wax and begin to decorate your candle. Continue using colours that go well together. When completed, use wax sealer to coat and protect your work.

1

2

2

2

Glass candleholder

Wax adheres to glass very well. The candle behind the image gives off a soft light and illuminates your design. A point to bear in mind, though, is that if your glass item is going to be used as a candleholder, which results in it getting hot from the flame, blow the candle out when you no longer want to use it, but **do not** touch the warm glass as it is sure to smudge. Rather wait until it has cooled completely before you touch it.

Requirements

- Paper design guide
- Glass candleholder
- Fabric marker
- Various coloured waxes
- Tissue (optional)
- Stylus
- Polyurethane, heat-resistant hard varnish and brush

1. Draw your design onto a piece of paper, roughly the same size as the design on the candleholder. This will be your guide. Place it inside the glass and use the fabric marker to draw the design onto the glass.

If you make a mistake, you can take a tissue and rub it off.

2. Turn the stylus on and dip the tip into the chosen wax colours, one at a time, and work on your design.

Continue until you have finished.

3. Paint a layer of polyurethane varnish over the painted area. This is a heat-resistant varnish and will help protect the wax from melting.

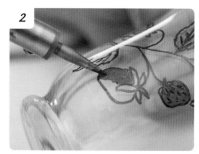

Glass candleholder with serviette

This project combines decoupage and encaustic to create a lovely centrepiece for a table. I have sealed the outside of the glass holder; firstly to give the background a very interesting texture and secondly, if the glass is quite thin, it is best to have a coat of heat-resistant, hard varnish to protect the wax. When choosing your picture, make sure it fits the object you are decorating.

Requirements

- Small glass candleholder
- Mulberry paper
- Polyurethane, heat-resistant hard varnish
- Paintbrush
- Serviette picture
- Scissors
- Clear and coloured wax
- Stylus

1. Tear the mulberry paper into small pieces. Paint a small area of the candleholder with the varnish (slightly larger than the torn paper piece) and press the mulberry paper onto the varnished area. Now, paint a layer of varnish over the mulberry paper, continuing in this way until the candleholder is completely covered. Allow to dry and repeat with another layer of varnish.

2. Cut out your serviette design and separate the layers. Turn the stylus on and, when hot, dip the drawing tip into the clear wax and attach the serviette by slowly drawing over the design. The serviette image will show through the clear wax.

3. Enhance the design on the serviette by adding accents with coloured wax using the stylus.

4. Once the picture is covered in wax, paint a layer of hard varnish over the serviette image.

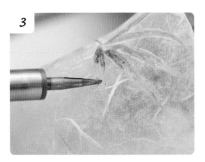

Sea shell painting

I have a collection of sea shells, gathered over the years from various holidays at the coast. Often these shells are all of a similar neutral colour and rather boring. I knew that they would make a good, absorbent base, so I decided to see how I could make them more interesting and colourful. If you do not have real shells you could always substitute by buying shells made from pottery and bisque fired. Use the technique previously described for ceramics (see page 108). You can varnish the shells when completed or leave them unvarnished.

Requirements

- Sea shells
- Stylus
- Various coloured waxes
- Dimensional gel or clear varnish (optional)

1. Make sure your shells are clean, and salt- and dust-free. They must be completely dry before you decorate them. Turn on the stylus and dip the drawing tip into shades of brown, white and clear wax. First make small square designs with the individual colours and fill in with the clear wax. This helps to blend and shade your colours.

2. You have some choices for final finishing. Either you can add dimensional gel to your shells, which gives them a high sheen and dimension, or you can varnish them. As these will be used for decoration purposes, you might like to leave them unvarnished to give them a matt finish, which can also be pretty.

HINT: If you do not know where to put the colour, either look up 'shells' on the Internet to find images, or copy a similar shell. The great thing about this project is you can paint the shells to suit the colour scheme in your bathroom, for example. You could also decorate them to add contrast to your original colour scheme.

Textures and mixed media

The term mixed media seems to have become highly fashionable these days. Whilst researching this book and chatting to fellow artists and crafters, I realised that the book would not be complete without featuring information on mixed media. I emphasize the word 'mixed' here because with this medium (encaustic) one can literally fuse anything to the warm wax! The reason you would choose textures is to create a three-dimensional piece of art. I have already spoken about the versatility of using tissue with wax, which is particularly effective as it takes on the colour you are working with whilst still giving a three-dimensional finish. Once you start adding 'bits' to your artwork, it opens up a whole new adventure and you begin to look at all sorts of things, wondering what they would look like on you picture. Sometimes you are successful and sometimes they don't work – that's the beauty of this art because it opens up a whole new, creative way of thinking.

I have used a multi-frame to display my different textures, which makes a lovely wedding or birthday gift. Try to assemble them using similar colours, as this gives an overall image of fluidity, creating the impression of one picture. So bear this in mind because clashing colours result in a disjointed look.

Bits and pieces

Many of us who have tried our hand at almost every craft known to mankind will be aware of the fact that we collect or, as I am guilty of, hoard lots and lots of bits and pieces, just to be used one day, maybe … just in case … With this type of artwork, you can use up plenty of different things to add texture or layer your picture. The other advantage an encaustic artist has over other artists is the fact that the wax used is already pigmented and adds translucency to the piece – although you will need a little bit of oil paint to add the finishing touches.

Feathers

Feathers are one of many items used to add texture. They work particularly well on canvas, for example, if you are doing a painting of a chicken or a bird, you could add the feathers in the places where they would appear on the bird. I use ostrich feathers, but any kind will do as they are soft and the wax adheres to them easily. You can use a single layer or multiple layers. Only add wax to the spine of the feather as this keeps the rest of the feather soft. If you add wax to the whole feather it ends up looking solid and rather plastic-like.

Feathers can also be used in abstracts to create points of interest in your picture.

Skeleton leaves

These leaves are easily obtainable from many craft or scrapbooking shops. The method is the same throughout the texture section of this book. I have used skeleton leaves very successfully when covering a jam jar, which was then used as a candle-holder. You may also stick the leaves to card; they make stunning occasion cards. I find the metallic colours work very well with this effect.

Dried flowers and leaves

Use flowers that you have dried yourself or obtain ready-dried flowers from craft shops. It is tricky using these delicate flowers and leaves as they break and tear very easily, so care must be taken when handling them.

I have made a panel for a scrapbook page using my dried flowers. This is a great way of adding interest when doing a page that requires a floral effect. Petals can have detail added to them by using the stylus.

The red roses were made from the casings of teabags. Twist them to form the petals, then adhere with a suitable colour wax, using the stylus.

Sand

Sand can be added to your seascape. This adds interest to your artwork as well as making the picture a little more realistic. When working with sand, be careful not to scratch the surface of your iron. To avoid this happening, lay the part of the picture that needs sand (for example the beach) over the iron, which you have assembled like a hot base plate. (See page 8 on iron assembly.) Then sprinkle the sand over the melted wax. You will have to pat it with your fingers to make sure it sticks, taking care not to burn yourself. Just remember: you will need a little more wax than usual to ensure that the sand has something to really stick to.

Gold leaf/powder/foil

The addition of either gold leaf or gold powder gives sparkle or finishing touches to some of your artworks. But do not use it on *all* of your projects. With experience, you will know what works with what. If you have worked with gold leaf, you will also know that it is a fairly tricky process!

Work with small areas at a time. Once you have completed your picture, apply a small amount of glue to the area you want to highlight. Use a glue pen – it's blue and available from art and craft shops. Let this glue dry for about 15 minutes. Now carefully place the gold leaf onto the glued area. You may have a few disasters before success (I certainly did!) but don't let this put you off – practise on scrap artwork instead of your beautiful masterpieces and you'll soon get the hang of it.

If you would like to start off with something a little easier, you can rather add foil to this tacky glue. This foil is normally bought at craft shops in the card making section. Place the underside of the foil to the glued area, rub firmly with your finger and lift off the foil. The gold or silver – or whatever colour your foil is – will now be transferred to the glue. Bear in mind that this is special crafting foil, not the tin foil you use in your kitchen!

Use the gold powder sparingly on the areas you want highlighted by simply putting a little on your finger and rubbing gently over those areas. You could also use a small, dry paint-brush, dipped into the powder and stroked on. You do not have to have any glue underneath this powder as it adheres to the waxed areas. If you use too much, it will cover the wax, so start off cautiously.

Sgraffito

After you have covered your card with wax, you can also use the scriber or an old credit card to make designs on it. Cut the edge of one of the sides of the credit card and scrape it over the card – this is called *sgraffito*. A comb may also be used for this effect. Put the card on an upturned iron in the hot-plate position before applying your effect.

Crushed paper effect

You get lovely effects when manipulating melted wax to create texture, and this is an easy technique.

1. Create a picture using the chaotic abstract method or simply lay wax on the card.

2. Crumple a piece of unprinted newspaper into a ball, open it up and place the slightly flattened piece of paper over your picture.

3. Place the iron over the flattened paper and slowly iron over it, lifting the opposite end as you do so. The sharp, crumpled edges cut through the wax – sometimes removing bits completely – leaving lines all over the picture.

4. Repeat this step if you are not happy with the result. You may find that you have to crush and iron your paper again.

5. Add highlights with gold powder if preferred (see alongside).

Tissue effect art

This is one of my favourite effects because I really enjoy adding texture to pictures. I have done this on small card as well as on canvas, and both supports are extremely effective.

Requirements

- Tissue – separated
- White A6 card
- Iron
- Clear candle wax
- Any two or three waxes
- Gold or silver metallic wax

1. Begin by crushing the separated, single-ply tissue into a ball. Open up the ball, maintaining the creases, and set aside. One tissue should be enough to cover the A6 card with a small amount of tissue overhanging the edges. This overhang will be used up when you pull the tissue towards the middle of your card to create the creases.

2. Now prepare the card by applying small amounts of clear candle wax onto the base of the heated iron and smoothing this wax onto the card. Then place the tissue onto the card and slowly iron over it, thereby securing it to the card.

3. Sculpt the tissue while it is still warm by laying your hand over it and pulling your hand gently inwards. As you do so, the tissue will begin to form raised creases.

HINT: Try not to be too rough as the tissue may tear. If this does happen it's not serious, as it will result in what I call bald patches – which is just another effect. You can patch up these areas by simply tearing a small piece of tissue and attaching it with a little candle wax.

4. Now you add the colours separately by melting a very small amount of encaustic wax onto the iron. Use circular movements to place the iron flat onto the area that you have chosen for that particular colour.

5. Repeat this process until you have covered the picture to your satisfaction. Lastly, take a gold or silver metallic wax and lightly add this to the base of the iron – not too much; add it carefully to avoid overdoing it. Using *no* pressure spread the iron over the creases of the tissue to highlight the raised areas. The weight of the iron will be enough to just touch the raised part of the tissue.

Note: The translucent waxes make this picture very effective as the clear wax under the tissue dilutes the pigment, diffusing the colour and actually blending and shading your picture to create a three-dimensional effect.

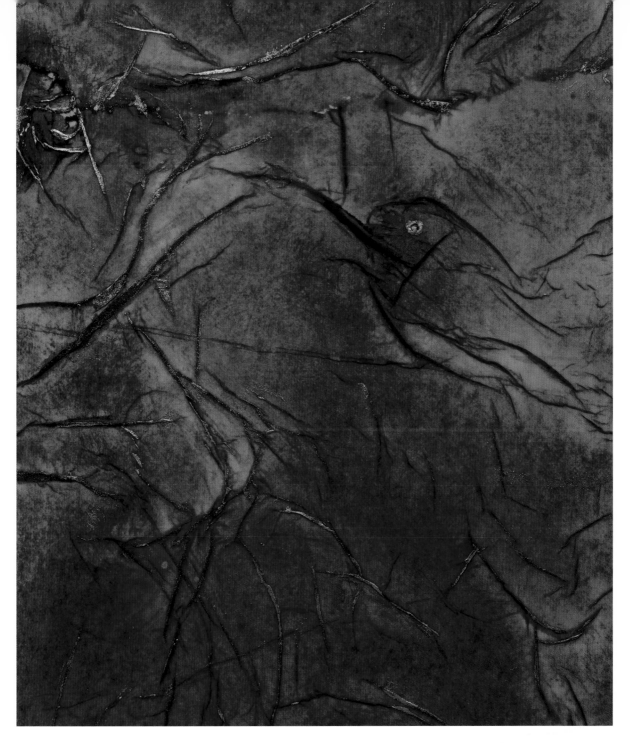

Encaustic on fabric

While you cannot do the basic encaustic techniques straight onto fabric, transferring encaustic designs from card gives a lovely texture, almost as if it has been painted onto a canvas support. I have transferred onto fabrics like calico, silk and quantec (tracksuit-type fabric) and found that silk works the best as the weave is fine and the picture stays clear and precise once transferred. Remember that your picture will be reversed once it has been transferred. Also choose a picture not too heavily loaded with wax, as the image may smudge during the transfer process.

Requirements

- Backing paper
- Encaustic picture
- White A6 card
- Fabric slightly bigger than card
- Tissue
- Iron
- Glue
- Window-frame card for finishing
- Spray mount

1. Cut your fabric 2,5 cm bigger than your picture (on all four sides) to provide you with enough extra fabric to wrap around the card.

2. Follow the diagram below of the order in which you should layer your tissue, fabric and picture.

3. Turn your iron onto a setting just beyond the low mark as the heat has to go through a few layers in order to transfer the wax.

4. Place the iron over the wax picture and hold it there for a few seconds, ensuring that you have applied heat to the entire picture. Slide the iron over the picture and simultaneously lift up the card from the corner where you started.

5. Spray the white card with spray mount and place it over the back of the fabric picture. Put clear glue onto the edges of the card and fold the fabric over so it sticks to the glue. Pull it tight so there are no creases and wait for it to dry. Place this in a window frame (or three-fold framed) card.

6. Do not discard the card that stays behind. It has a lovely texture and can also be used either with the fabric transfer or on its own.

- Iron
- Encaustic picture facing downwards
- Fabric (right side up)
- Tissue
- Backing paper

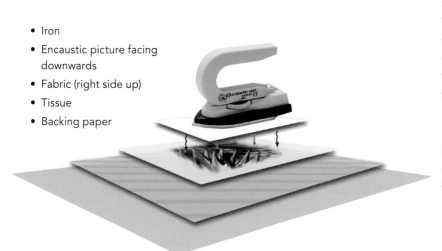

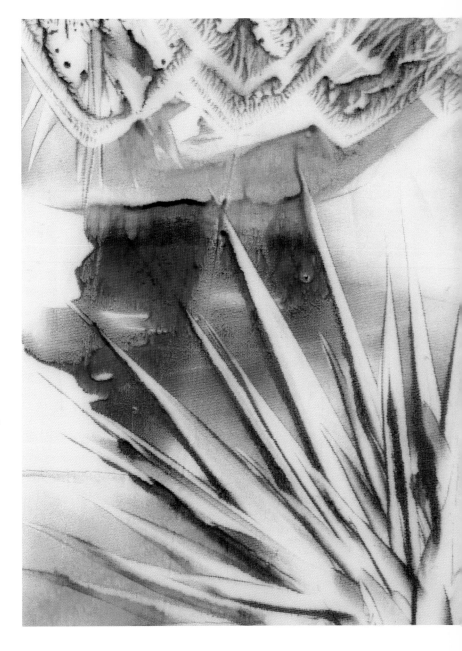

Note: A window-frame card is a card that has three sections. A 'window' is cut from the middle section and the picture placed behind the opening. Then the right-hand section is folded over and glued to cover the back of the picture, giving the card a neat, clean finish.

Mixed media collage

You can use either canvas or MDF. I tend to use ready-to-hang framed boards bought at a craft shop and would suggest you use something similar, as canvas can be expensive, especially when you are still a beginner at this.

1. Melt beeswax on the upturned iron or directly on the hot tray. Dip the brush into the wax and coat the entire board, quite thickly.

2. Heat with a heat gun or iron to fuse. As soon as the wax starts to shine, move quickly to the next area or you may lift the wax off with too much heat.

3. Using your iron, melt the wax on area where you want to place the theme picture, lay the picture into the melted wax and press down firmly with your hand. Paint a layer of wax over the picture and reheat to fuse.

4. Tear small amounts of scrunched-up tissue paper and place these onto your board around the images. Now melt beeswax over the tissue paper with the iron. Add colour all around the pictures by melting a small amount of coloured wax on the tip of the iron to position.

5. Attach feathers by melting a line of wax with the side of the iron and placing it on the vein or spine of the feather, pressing down with your

Requirements

- Wooden framed board
- Beeswax pellets
- Brush (not nylon)
- Encaustic wax
- Theme picture printed on office paper, or wraping paper
- Tissue paper
- Wrapping paper with similar themed pictures
- Guinea fowl feathers, sculptured animals, tea bag paper, handmade paper, gold leaves, lace, netting, stamped image cut out,
- Glue
- Hot tray or iron in hot tray position
- Iron
- Heat gun
- Wax sealer

Little steps for little paws
Always playtime
In the great outdoors

6

6

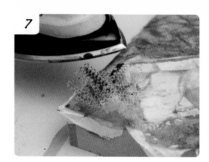

7

8

9

hand to secure. This way the feather still has a light, fluffy look. If you put too much wax over the feather, it will look like plastic. Now attach the other elements.

6. Assemble your collage and attach all the lighter embellishments securely with wax.

7. Melt a small amount of coloured wax on the tip of the iron and dab this wax over the areas around your pictures and embellishments taking care not to go over the picture.

8. Load a small amount of gold wax onto the base of the iron and lightly spread over the textured areas thus highlighting the creases.

9. Enhance the lettering on the pattern paper using brown wax and the stylus.

10. Finally glue the heavier charms into position.

Note: Feather the edges of your theme pictures to avoid harsh straight lines. This is done by wetting the outside of you picture with water and when it has soaked in pull the paper away with your fingers creating a feathered edge.

Other items you can add include

- Bandage gauze – various types
- Lace
- Buttons
- Beads
- Metal shapes (these can be used to press and stamp into your wax layers)
- Old dress patterns
- Postage stamps
- Hair clips (Kirby grips)
- The casings of tea bags

10

Wax on wood

The example I show here is very simple. You can use a stylus to do a number of designs onto raw wood. The wax is a good medium to use for this application, as the wooden surface absorbs it. The flower I used as an embellishment I made with air-dried clay, using the stylus to add colour with encaustic wax.

Requirements

- Wooden item with a smooth surface
- Pencil
- Design
- Stylus
- Brown wax
- Embellishments
- Wood glue

1. Draw your design very lightly in pencil onto the piece of wood. Turn the stylus on with the drawing tip attached, dip it into the brown wax and draw over your pencilled image. Continue until you have finished your design.

HINT: If the wooden item is small, like mine, keep it simple and do not overload it with too much detail.

2. Glue your embellishments onto the wood with wood glue. I have added a small bee as well as a sunflower that I made out of clay. The clay I used was air-dried clay, which can be bought from a craft shop. I then covered the flower with wax, using the stylus. You could do something similar that matches the image you are putting onto the wood.

Templates

Enlarge to fit the size of your intended support and project

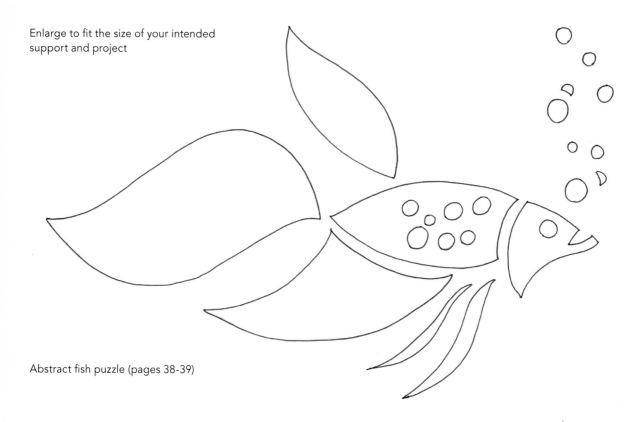

Abstract fish puzzle (pages 38-39)

Mother's Day card (pages 72-73)

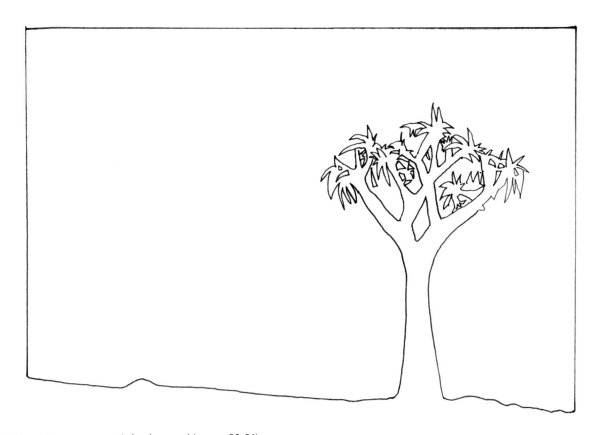

Silhouettes on encaustic background (pages 90-91)

Mother's Day card (pages 72-73)

Silhouettes on encaustic background
(pages 90-91)

Acknowledgements

I would like to thank my husband Carl, son Ian and daughter Lauren (fondly known as Floss) for all their support, encouragement, patience and – most of all – believing in me whilst I was writing this book. I would never have accomplished this dream without them. They were always there to lend an ear, be my critics and share ideas. As new ideas came to mind they would listen enthusiastically and give advice, both positive or negative. I would like to give Floss a special thank you for lending me her expertise in Photoshop, thereby helping me to produce such clear and decisive graphics in my book.

Thanks must also go to my sister Joanie, who introduced me to Encaustic Art in the first place some fourteen years ago in Zimbabwe. Had it not been for her, I may never have discovered this amazing art form and, consequently, this book would never have been published. I only wish that my late father had still been around to witness the writing and publishing of my book – I hope he would have been proud of me. Thanks too to Mum and sisters Les and Debs for all their wonderful words of encouragement and never giving up on me.

I have very fond memories of the late Keith Thurman who was an importer of encaustic equipment. I worked with Keith for ten years as his agent and had a special and unique working relationship with him and his wife Manuella.

I would like to express my gratitude to Monique Day-Wilde who has given me endless advice and help during the writing of my book. I would also like to acknowledge Wilsia, Lindie and Liezl of Metz Press for publishing my book: thanks for all the help, advice and encouragement that you have given me. Lastly, thank you Ivan Naudé for the absolutely gorgeous photography. You make my work look amazing.

Readers who require further information on encaustic art or the equipment used for the projects in this book are welcome to contact me at *jannvisser@gmail.com.*

Frame with compliments of Rosendal Galerie 021 976 8232